Release From Isolation

RELEASE FROM

J. S. MARTINDALE

Associate Chairman, Department of Psychology
Northeastern Illinois State College

ISOLATION:

How to find FRIENDSHIP, LOVE, AND HAPPINESS

NELSON-HALL COMPANY CHICAGO

ISBN 911012-08-7

Library of Congress Catalog Card No. 79-162932

Nelson-Hall Co., Publishers
325 W. Jackson Blvd., Chicago, Ill. 60606

Manufactured in the United States of America

Although the examples in this book are based upon the behavior of real people, the names have been changed, along with other significant biographical information, to protect the identity of persons living or dead.

To Patricia

Contents

Acknowledgments

I have been strongly influenced in my beliefs by Hubert Bonner, former Professor of Humanistic Psychology at United States International University in San Diego, and Carl Rogers, fellow of The Center for the Studies of the Person, at La Jolla, California.

I also owe much to the work of Fritz Perls, the father of gestalt therapy, and Gardner Murphy, whose lifelong work I admire greatly. The most important works by these men – to my mind – are listed in the suggested readings at the end of the book.

J. Stanley Martindale, Ph.D.

Introduction

Reliable evidence reveals that one out of every four Americans needs or will need mental therapy at some point in his life. Right now, more hospital beds are occupied by patients suffering primarily from emotional disorders than by those with physical diseases or ailments. And the number with emotional problems increases steadily. How does the average person work through this emotional wilderness?

A popular myth has it that a person needs a trained expert to lead him to mental health, happiness, and personal success. The myth insists that the person needs therapy, and lots of it. He is urged on all sides, by relatives, friends, or employers, to seek help from a psychiatrist, psychologist, or some other professional in a related field. And if he follows this advice, it may easily be his first mistake.

I believe the conventional approach of one-to-one therapy, where the patient is locked in with an expert in a dependent relationship, is largely a failure, and has been since its inception. It seldom is successful for the patient even after long treatment. It does work well for many therapists, however, who pocket substantial fees in the interim.

Furthermore, I believe that most currently fashionable group techniques are outdated, inadequate, and usually mis-

11

leading. More on this later. The fact is, many troubled persons do not need individual guidance from a therapist. The troubled person usually can help himself, provided he can learn to understand his problem and master certain techniques to use in coping with his dilemma. And this is the purpose of this book: To help provide the self-taught skills with which a person can relieve emotional pain, understand how he got the way he is, and know what to do if change is desired.

Psychology may be in difficulty

If what is real and true in psychology can't be taught to the average person so that he can use this knowledge to find his healthy processes on his own, then psychology is in serious difficulty. Every recent outgoing president of the American Psychological Association has struck the warning note that psychologists are supporting the myth of professional magic, and lining their pockets more than aiding people in trouble.

Let me illustrate this point. A young woman of twenty, let's call her Ellen, had long felt she was a little more disturbed than the average person. She was plagued by unpleasant memories of past experiences, and by real doubt that she was "normal." She worried about her strong feelings about a dead stepfather, and about her sexual feelings for her best girl friend.

A combination of these two worries plagued her relationship with the young man with whom she shared an apartment. A mental picture of her dead stepfather would pop into her mind's eye during a passionate embrace, for instance. And she was uncomfortable when with her best girl friend.

So, Ellen went to a conventional psychologist, who told her that she would need long-term treatment. He began probing her past family conflicts—her Freudian past—indicating that it was here that the "cure" would be found. This is the beginning of a failed technique.

Ellen was an aggressive young woman full of anxiety expressed as fears and guilts. She was an absolutely normal woman. The things that were plaguing her were *current* in her unfinished emotional life and were attempting to emerge into awareness in her day-to-day existence. She had to learn how to let these unresolved emotional experiences bubble to the surface where she could understand what they were and work them through.

She learned (within a week) to work through her unpleasant memories, to recreate them as if each situation were occurring for the first time, to pretend the experience was happening right now, and to get in touch with what was still unfinished in her emotional needs surrounding the memory.

Ellen could not bear to go near the room in her home where her stepfather died. In working through the unpleasant memories of this room, she discovered she had wanted her stepfather to embrace her, and that she had been feeling guilty about this for the three years since his death. Ellen made this discovery on her own while sitting quietly at home and working through her feelings.

More discoveries follow

This discovery led her to yet another unfinished emotional need. She discovered she hated her mother, and blamed her for divorcing Ellen's real father. Ellen faced her mother and verbally expressed her very strong feelings about this. And this in turn, led her to understand her feelings about her girl friend, and that she had a physical attraction for her. This did not matter, even though the friend was pretty, because Ellen preferred men.

Ellen discovered that her need to be physically close to a father could be filled quite easily by being near her boy friend's father, who kissed and hugged her as if she were his own daughter. She achieved a deep and satisfying relationship with her mother. And her affair with her boy friend took on new dimensions.

As with Ellen, you may discover that my first objective is *to help you get in touch with yourself.* You can do this by reliving your past experiences — whether they were pleasant or unpleasant — as though they were happening right now.

Then, you can learn to find friendship, love, and sexual happiness through small *gestalt groups*. (These are not to be confused with the many varieties of "encounter groups" now in vogue.) I shall carefully develop these themes by means of case histories of real people and through detailed explanations and suggestions.

A word of caution: As you read, do not be discouraged if at first you don't find instant answers to your emotional dilemma. I do not offer an alphabetical list of emotional hangups and solutions to which you may refer as in a dictionary. Indeed, as you proceed, you may feel you are working out a jigsaw puzzle. Gradually, the pieces may fall into place, and eventually form a "picture" to which you can relate your own special problem. That is, you may begin to relate the case studies to your own experience and to work out things for yourself. You "put it all together" on your own.

What is a gestalt group?

Since the success of your efforts will depend largely on how well you relate to gestalt groups, it may be helpful to have a clear understanding of what they are. Broadly, a *gestalt group* is any natural gathering of persons, whether by geography, occupation, social organization, friendship, marriage — any of the groups in which persons come together, formally or informally, for some period of time. An *artificial group* is gathering or collection of persons, who are strangers, for some specific task or purpose not supported by other relationships *outside the group effort*. A group created by design to bring persons together to have a "group experience" is an artificial group, not a gestalt group.

A family may be a gestalt group. A group of neighborhood friends, a circle of business associates, acquaintances who meet regularly for lunch, students who come together in a classroom, a group of patients in touch with one another in a hospital, and coworkers may all be gestalt groups.

Almost any kind of informal or formal grouping of persons may exhibit what is meant here by gestalt group. It is not intended to be an inflexible category. What *is* intended is to point out the very heavy, nearly-always-fatal burden facing those artificial groups that are formed to have a group experience and lack the cohesive support of a broader network of human relationships among members. When persons leave an artificial group session, they go their separate ways and are isolated from further contact with one another.

My own research with small groups this past eight years has led me to believe that what happens or can happen in gestalt groups as contrasted with what occurs in the more artificial kinds of groups is so different that the processes should be examined most carefully. There is strong evidence that there is an existing body of knowledge and certain skills that can be learned to aid in our search for awareness through our inner feelings as we come together in small groups.

Awareness of the processes of change and growth in a person could become the aim of any gestalt group. This involves learning how you feel about yourself, and others, and the world outside. Most of us are nearly totally out of contact with our feelings, and in a condition of low-grade emergency where it is difficult for us to discover or enjoy good, close contact with others and to communicate how we feel.

Aware and unaware behavior

Gestalt groups may be used to help a person break through this pattern of pain, on the assumption that nothing can be done unless a person first becomes aware of what's happening to his feelings. There is no unconscious or subconscious behavior in gestalt psychology. There is *aware* and *unaware* behavior. Behavior that you are not aware of is simply below your threshold of awareness, deep in the background — the ground — of your experience. The goal of gestalt groups could be to aid the process of awareness through roleless behavior. To describe how this may be done is a purpose of this book.

Perhaps the central theme or philosophy underlying my effort in this book is the belief that persons should be taught to adjust their environment to fit themselves, not to "adjust" themselves to fit their environment. The passive person, who waits on external events to shape him, or show him how to be, pays a heavy price.

There is a serious misunderstanding of how a person survives, grows, and lives a healthy life. Most of us are reared to believe that external events are largely responsible for what we are, that impersonal "objective" processes mold us beyond change or repair. The belief that our parents (or "society" or "man" or "destiny") made us what we are nearly immobilizes the healing and integrating life forces constantly seeking self-expression in a person.

Roleless behavior is natural

The natural condition of a person is roleless behavior — behavior that wants to absorb and assimilate the inner needs of a person with his outside world. Role behavior, the social guidelines of how to behave, does not allow the person to experience that behavior as his own. Role behavior belongs to someone else and it alienates the person until he can find what portions of it fit himself. Role behavior must be torn down, remade, and assimilated in the affective behavior of a person before he can feel it is his own and belongs to him.

Roleless behavior organizes the person to respond to his survival needs. It is the person's unifying, integrating way of being. Conventional psychology has failed for many years to find ways of teaching the average person how and what to do to enjoy good emotional health. A major purpose in writing this book is to describe what a person can do to create warm human groups for himself and discard or change those artificial relationships where persons interact in sterile, rolebound rituals.

1

How to Avoid Therapy
and the Personality Trap

Conventional therapy leads into a personality trap. The following case history illustrates this point: Mr. and Mrs. John Jones were plagued by continuing conflict in their marriage of ten years. The tension seemed to be greatest over the spending of money. Mary Jones liked to save money because money in the bank gave her a deep sense of security.

John Jones preferred to spend money on material "necessities" or activities because this gave him a deep sense of security. John liked to buy a new car every year because he felt it would be safe and would run well. Mary preferred to drive an older car and keep the money in the bank for emergencies.

Both Mary and John Jones had ways of handling money that were directly linked with their own deep personal needs for security. Conventional therapy, which supports the myth of personality, attempted to persuade these persons to adjust themselves to fit new goals as husband and wife, such as agreeing to buy a new car every two or three years instead of annually.

This "adjustment" satisfied neither John nor Mary. The original conflict was still there, barely papered over. Each partner still had an unfinished emotional conflict about his own personal need for security. The way each was attempting to adjust to personal security needs in the first place was artificial, and the compromise failed.

The new goal of buying a car every two years compounded the error of the original adjustment. The new adjustment was in opposition to the healthy process. A healthful solution would have resulted when both Mary and John adjusted their ways of doing things as husband and wife to fit their own real and individual needs.

The way of spending or not spending money was a mask covering the real human needs of John and Mary. Therapy works when the person is taught to abandon those parts of his personality that do not fulfill his real needs.

For Mary, it might have been as straightforward as getting pregnant and having a baby to care for. Or, it may have been that she needed to get rid of the responsibility of caring for the children she already had.

For John, it might have been that he needed another job that fitted him better. Or, maybe he really didn't want to work at all, and would rather have traveled around doing as he pleased. Mary and John did not have an easy solution to their conflict.

And conventional therapy seldom helps. Whether the therapy is the traditional private arrangement or the more modern group session, it tends to support the myth of personality. This elaborate myth is founded on the idea that your personality is the real you.

The myth of the "well-adjusted personality"

There has always been the best of evidence that your personality is merely an artificial reproduction of yourself which you have created to use as your social behavior — and that this sometimes awkward personality you create interferes with your genuine behavior and good mental health.

We are on ground sacred to traditionalists, therefore I will proceed with care. The "well-adjusted personality" seems to be a national goal. Conventional therapy, individual or group, attempts to get you to adjust yourself to fit your personality instead of getting you to adjust your personality to fit yourself, the real you.

This involves a serious misunderstanding of human behavior. Conventional therapy assumes that you should adjust yourself to fit your personality in spite of the fact that when this occurs, personal alienation gets worse. John and Mary Jones are a typical example of a failed marriage in which the partners attempted to adjust themselves to fit roles that didn't fulfill real needs. Attempting to induce you to adjust yourself to fit your personality instead of training you how to adjust your personality to fit the real you is similar to trying to wear a shoe that is too small for your foot. No matter how many size nines you try out, if you need a size ten, you had best adjust the size of the shoe to fit your foot.

In John and Mary Jones' case, each had a need for personal security that was not being satisfied in their roles as husband and wife. To try to get them to adjust their need for security within their old roles would not work. They must adjust their roles to fit their security needs.

Natural and social behavior

The myth of the "well-adjusted personality" seems so strong as to be impossible to demolish. You have two very different kinds of behavior. One is the *natural behavior* of the self. The other is the *social behavior* you learn after you are born. Social behavior is *role behavior,* and natural behavior is *roleless.*

Now, each person is born with tendencies to be integrated, over-integrated, or under-integrated with his social behavior, or his "personality of roles." I am using the term *integrate* to describe a person's capacity to unify biologically inherited behavior with learned social behavior.

Let me illustrate. An infant is born without any social behavior. He soon begins to learn the social behavior of how to eat. As this infant matures, he is taught certain group ways of handling his food while eating and drinking; that is, he learns to use knives, forks, spoons, plates, and cups. At first, these ways of handling food while eating are roles.

Many of these learned ways of behaving "fit" the infant. He adopts these group ways first as roles, and then absorbs them as his own genuine natural behavior. He integrates his social behavior with his natural behavior.

The integration process

The process of integration is his absorbing these group ways of social behavior to the point where they become part of his natural behavior. Many group ways of behaving with food may fit the infant. But some of these ways may not be absorbed as part of his natural behavior. Still, the infant is persuaded to adopt them anyway as the proper, social way to act. That behavior which the infant doesn't integrate as his own becomes his "personality," that is, his social behavior (personality of social behavior).

For example, the infant may quickly absorb (integrate) how to eat with a spoon. He may not learn how to eat with a fork as quickly and as well. He must be drilled to act in those ways that don't come naturally to him. Eventually he will develop "table manners" of how to eat with a fork, although he does not absorb using a fork as part of his natural behavior. Using a fork is part of his social behavior, or personality. This portion of his table manners is a counterfeit of his natural behavior.

We tend to follow our natural behavior because it is spontaneous and unrehearsed. We don't need to rehearse "what comes naturally." But that part of our behavior which we have not integrated as our own becomes our social behavior (personality) and for this behavior we have to rehearse. We silently rehearse our actions, and plan what we are going to do or say. *Whenever you have to silently rehearse before you act or talk, you are "adjusting" yourself to fit your personality, and are not functioning with your natural behavior.* Your natural behavior is spontaneous and integrated. You don't need to "think it over" first.

Think a moment. When you talk to yourself, who is doing the talking? When you scold yourself, or urge, nag, plead, demand, direct, or command yourself, who is this perfectionist? Who is silently rehearsing you before you act or talk? You, of course.

This verbal replica of yourself is your personality in action, attempting to adjust your natural behavior to the social behavior of your personality. This spokesman for your social behavior attempts to translate your natural behavior into words so that you can act within your personality of social behavior. For example, you meet a stranger for the first time at a social gathering. Your first impression may be that you do not like this stranger. But you smile, and shake hands, and say, "How nice to meet you." That's your personality in action, a counterfeit of your natural behavior (which is what you really feel about the stranger). And you have to be careful with "yourself" and not reveal what you really think about the stranger. You rehearse your response to make sure you don't say what you think.

Suppose you like the stranger at first glance. You are in a personality trap here, too; you still smile and shake hands and play the "how-nice-to-meet-you" role of social behavior. Your personality of social behavior is a mask of your natural behavior. In both of these instances, a role of social behavior is used to conceal your true response to the stranger.

The integrated person

Most persons live too much within their personality of social behavior. They tend to be either under-integrated or over-integrated. The over-integrated person tends to have too much social behavior and the under-integrated person too little. *An integrated person has a balance of natural behavior and social behavior.*

As long as you are aware that the roles of social behavior you play are not your genuine behavior, you won't suffer a serious "personality" disorder. But most persons come to believe the myth of personality: that the personality is the real self. And they attempt to cram their natural behavior into this contrived structure of personality roles.

Actually, many persons are aware of the differences between their natural and social behavior and say that they have "split personalities." In reality, what seems to be true is that they are recognizing the fundamental difference between their personality, which is their social behavior, and their natural behavior.

The over-integrated person

As I stated earlier, most persons have too much or too little personality (social behavior). Let me describe over-integrated and under-integrated persons. George was a young man just starting college. He had been a good student, earning high grades all through high school, and had never caused any trouble. In fact, he seemed to his friends and parents to be too careful, too cautious. He was extremely neat about everything, usually very polite, and seldom displayed anger.

But George didn't make close friends. When he was nineteen, his parents noticed that he appeared to be suffering, and behaved in ways different from the usual. He spent more and more time alone. He talked less and less.

George was over-integrated in social behavior. He had too much personality. He did not seem to be very emotional. He was too rigid with himself. He wouldn't take chances—he always tried to find the safe way to go. He seemed too self-controlled. Girls didn't take to him, and he had no lasting friendships.

All of a sudden, George seemed to fall apart. Drastic and rapid change became visible. He moved away from home and joined a group of nonstudents who seemed to be living the worst kind of life. This situation didn't end well for George or his parents. All were alienated and couldn't find a way to resolve their differences. George blamed himself. The parents blamed themselves, and wondered where they "went wrong." Also, each partly blamed the other. A circular trap; a zero game in which no one could win.

Neither the parents nor George were at "fault." It was a serious mistake for any of these persons to blame each other or themselves. This family was living the myth of personality. Each was attempting to adjust to fit a role of mother or father or son, instead of modifying the role to fit individual needs.

This family did not learn how to find roles to fit the individual person. They were suffering great pain by being alienated from one another while caring deeply for each other. It was as if they were all swimming under water together but could barely hear, touch, or see each other. Basic human needs of love, care, affection, and security cannot be satisfied if persons interact with one another through their personalities. This is a major dilemma.

George was born with a tendency to over-integrate in social behavior. He adopted so much social behavior that he couldn't absorb it all as his own genuine behavior. To explain how this dilemma occurs and what to do about it is one of the main purposes of this book. You will hear more about it as we go along.

The under-integrated person

Let's take another example. It concerns a young woman of eighteen, whom I'll call Carol. She tended to be an under-integrated person, one with too little personality (social behavior). Her parents considered her to be a walking, talking, social disaster. She was utterly disorganized. Her room was a cluttered mess. She had no sense of direction, whether east, west, north, or south. When she finally got off to work, she looked as if she had dressed in her closet in the dark.

Carol was always behind, racing to catch up with herself. Her life seemed to be a series of unfinished situations, one after another. Certain words fitted her exactly: disorganized, scatterbrained, flighty, too emotional. She had been fired or gently "let go" from several jobs. Carol was miserable, and like George, visibly suffered.

George over-integrated into social behavior, that is, he adopted too many group ways of doing things. The group ways of doing things are adopted as roles until they are absorbed as part of the natural behavior of the person. George adopted too many roles and couldn't absorb them all; most of the roles he took up didn't fit him, and he couldn't adjust himself to fit his personality of roles no matter how much he tried.

Carol had the opposite problem. She was under-integrated in her social behavior, or personality of roles. She had not learned enough roles with which to practice until she found what fit her natural behavior. She hadn't learned that roles are a vehicle through which persons discover what behavior fits them best.

Integrated persons use roles

An integrated person has neither too many nor too few personality roles. He is balanced between his natural behavior, or individuality, and his social behavior. The integrated person uses roles to accommodate strangers, to get along with large numbers of persons in a crowd, or while engaged in activities such as driving a car on a highway.

The integrated person uses roles to enable him to be formal and to keep others at a distance until he chooses to have a more personal relationship. He uses roles to get by in situations in which he doesn't know how to act. But he always "buys shoes to fit his feet." He doesn't use a role that is too big or too small. The integrated person uses roles deliberately, and is aware that they are not his genuine behavior, but his social behavior, to be discarded when he wants others to respond to his basic human needs.

Over-integrated George is what I call *role-bound*, and under-integrated Carol is *roleless*. An integrated person is largely roleless, but does have a few roles he uses when he needs them.

Carol and her family, like George and his, were caught in the personality trap, the myth that individuals in families can develop "well-adjusted personalities," that each member can adjust himself to fit whatever he believes to be the "well-adjusted personality."

An integrated person does not have a "well-adjusted personality." He is largely roleless and is aware of when he is using his social behavior. A man of about thirty, let's call him Charles, is a good example. When Charles met a stranger and was not sure whether or not he liked him on first impression, he merely nodded, confirming that they were meeting one another. If Charles met someone he liked at first glance, he found a way to express his reaction. He might shake hands and say, "I'm glad to meet you; let's talk later if we can."

Charles acted *with his experience.* His social expressions and behavior were in agreement with how he felt about himself and others around him. He knew he didn't have to say anything to a stranger he didn't care for. Just because he felt something didn't mean he must act on this feeling. *He acted with his experience.* His meeting with the stranger was a felt experience. And nearly always this may be sensed by the other person in the encounter. Nothing big, but this is how an integrated person stays in touch with himself.

Neither Carol nor George had many felt experiences, and this led to a sense of alienation. All of the little or big things they did were attempts to adjust themselves to fit a personality of roles. And being either over-integrated or under-integrated, they needed to be taught how to adjust roles to fit themselves, to fit their own unique tendencies of natural behavior.

What to do is important

This book attempts to show *what* to do to become a healthy individual. *Why* persons are the way they are is not my direct concern. You may have a thousand reasons or explanations of why you got the way you are. Knowing why doesn't help. Once you discover the *what* and *how,* all the *whys* probably will fall into place.

Most persons are born with tendencies to become either over- or under-integrated with social behavior. They have been influenced in how they developed their personality of social behavior and integrated it with their natural behavior.

These influences come from all the various groups of persons around one (family, friends, and acquaintances) and from books, movies, and television. A feral person, one who grows up wild, out of contact with a human group, would be role-less. He would not have learned any roles. He would have no personality. All of his behavior would be natural behavior, but he wouldn't be able to fit in any social group in any society.

The feral person wouldn't know a language or how to cooperate with others to live as a member of their group. You may know someone who seems more feral than social, but even the worst outlaw has some social behavior that separates him from a true feral person, who would not even talk, for he would know no languages.

You also may know someone who has become over-integrated and seems to be a social robot, an automated, mechanical man who talks too much. He is all talk-talk; he talks about talk, spoken or written talk, but it is not *felt* talk. This urban robot seems hardly more human than the feral person, and appears lost in a verbal wilderness, communicating with no one.

But I use extreme examples to illustrate a point. *Social behavior is role behavior. Natural behavior is roleless.* Your social behavior is your personality of roles and your natural behavior is the real you.

The importance of roles

You learned roles while a member of some human group. The roles you absorbed as your own behavior are **not** part of the natural behavior of your self. The roles you did not absorb are part of your personality of social behavior. You may have too many or too few roles, depending on whether you are an under- or over-integrated person. The great majority of persons tend to be one or the other. A few have integrated themselves.

Let's take a look at how an under-integrated person and an over-integrated person discovered behavior that helped them to become integrated persons. These case histories provide working definitions of terms which, on first reading, may appear somewhat abstract.

The anomic personality

Under-integrated persons tend to create for themselves what I call an *anomic* (a-nom-ik) personality. Anomic is derived from the French word *anomie,* which means normlessness, or without many group ways. The over-integrated person tends to develop a *verbal* personality. The verbal personality uses words or thinking to replace real behavior. (I describe both of these types of personalities at length in later chapters.)

Jane was an under-integrated woman of thirty-eight, who had an anomic personality. She had always felt awkward and clumsy. She felt unfeminine in the way she walked. Jane had an acquaintance, Martha, whom she didn't know too well, but admired because of the way she walked. It seemed so female and graceful.

Jane was urged to find out what Martha did to walk the way she did. Not why, but the specific details of how and what she did when she walked. Jane got up enough courage to ask, and Martha was surprised but delighted to help if she could. She thought it over and demonstrated how she learned her walk. When she was about eleven, Martha remembered, she found she could walk the way she wanted by starting a step, gliding halfway through, and then finishing her stride. Step and glide, step and glide. Martha practiced this walking role, absorbed it as her own within a few minutes, and retained and perfected it to her satisfaction.

Jane watched how Martha walked, practiced, and very quickly found this way of walking fit her, too. She changed her way of walking immediately. She had found a fit, a way of walking that suited her perfectly.

For our second example, we'll take a young man who was over-integrated and had developed a verbal personality. This man's handwriting was all but illegible. He had had great difficulty with his handwriting all through school and was still disappointed in it. A meticulous, neat person, he wanted very much to write with a precise hand.

Now, no one had been able to help him discover how to improve or change his writing. Many teachers had given him reasons why he wrote so poorly, but none of this helped, and at twenty he still couldn't read his own writing at times.

This young man, we'll call him Steve, was encouraged to find someone who wrote the way Steve wanted to, and ask that person how he did it. Steve had a friend whose writing was beautiful, and Steve asked him for help. Steve's friend sat down and wrote a few pages while Steve watched. Steve kept asking him to break down each little motion and explain how he wrote as he did. This suggestion didn't seem to get them anywhere. Finally Steve sat next to his friend and attempted to copy exactly how he held a pencil and how he wrote. Discovery!

Steve noticed that his friend held the pencil higher in the grip of his fingers than Steve did. Steve practiced a moment and realized that he was gripping his pencil nearly at the lead and that his fingers concealed what he was writing. He found that he could not see how he was forming words as he wrote. In other words, he couldn't see what he was writing.

Steve had learned to write early in his life and was too rigid to experiment once he had mastered a "role" he was taught. All of these years he thought he was writing in a way that was his own. But, as with Jane in the previous example. he had deep dissatisfaction with himself. Neither Jane's walk nor Steve's writing had been absorbed as their own genuine natural behavior.

The meaning of gestalt

We learn roles, our social behavior, as members of some small personal group. I call these small personal groups *gestalt* (guh-shtalt') groups. Gestalt is a German word meaning the process of a form or pattern emerging or taking shape. There is no precise English translation. Your family, a close circle of friends, a small group of office coworkers, a neighborhood group — all of these are gestalt groups.

Your gestalt groups are all of the small groups of persons of which you are a member and with which you have established some kind of personal bond. Gestalt groups arise out of the social network of your personal relationships, whatever their origins. Your gestalt groups generally have two, three, four, or five persons, counting yourself. Steve and Jane in the examples above made their discoveries in their own gestalt groups.

You usually create your own personality from roles you have adopted while a member of your personal gestalt groups: your family, your circle of friends, and sometimes more casual acquaintances. You also discover ways of personality change within your gestalt groups.

Most of your deep personal needs are gratified in gestalt groups. Love, care, affection, sex, joy, happiness, security — all are found in gestalt groups. Most persons do not have enough gestalt groups. Some do not have any at times in their lives. Another chapter is devoted to the dynamics and processes of these gestalt groups.

Natural and artificial groups

Just as there are two kinds of personal behavior, (natural and social behavior), there are two basic kinds of human groups in relation to an individual. There are natural groups, which I call gestalt groups. And there are artificial groups, where persons come together for some reason but do not interact *except* with their personalities, that is, with their social behavior.

These artificial groups hardly need description. Most persons live mostly within artificial groups in which everyone seems to relate only superficially to each other, through their personalities of roles, or social behavior. No real, personal bonds are established, and the persons in these artificial groups have artificial experiences. These are counterfeit relationships.

You cannot develop a personal bond with another person by using your personality. You establish personal bonds when both you and the other person are acting with your experience of one another, each in concert with his own needs. This is natural behavior.

The "encounter group" phenomenon

Both anomic and verbal personalities are drawn to the encounter group phenomenon, which has captured the imagination of people nearly everywhere. Both anomic and verbal personalities lack adequate personal gestalt groups. They are attracted to a variety of popular group forms that have as many names as there are practitioners: encounter groups, sensitivity groups, learning groups, training groups, love groups, marathon groups, and on and on—anything that promises to satisfy their hunger for emotional release or renewal.

These artificial "pop" groups are not just a fad. They are responses to real human needs. But they have serious flaws. They are artificial groups and their very organization invites artificial experiences. They almost always have a leader (trainer, guide) who directs the group action. He gives the group specific things to do, such as games to play. This is an authoritarian role relationship that invites a role response; the other persons in the group must take on the role of "good group members."

My own research and work with small groups these past several years, includes both what I call the natural gestalt group and the artificial kind of group. The difference in what happens between these two kinds of groups is so great that I will return to them at length in later chapters.

For now, let me offer one example. As noted earlier, these artificial groups attract both anomic and verbal personalities, who generally do not have enough warm, personal, natural gestalt groups of their own. They usually have isolated and partial friendships with a few persons, one here and one there. They seldom have a circle of friends of even three to five members, and rarely have close relationships with even one or two members of their family.

Both the anomic and verbal personality have problems that are based upon their inability to act with their natural behavior, to express their "self" adequately with another person. To illustrate, let me recreate part of a group session. One member, Maxine, was a woman of thirty-five, and an anomic personality. She wanted to learn how to understand her son better, and perhaps improve her relationship with her husband. There were no integrated persons in the group, which was a mixture of some verbal and some anomic personalities, with more anomics than verbals. A male with a verbal personality took over. Let's call him Joe. And then began the personality trap.

This was an artificial group. The persons had gathered to have an "experience." First, there were too many present to attract natural responses. The group had ten members. Groups of over five tend to invite formal personality behavior.

But the personality trap was that Maxine and the others had to adjust themselves to fit the group. They were not able to adjust the group to fit themselves. Maxine, with an anomic personality, a "weak" role structure, was nearly helpless to respond to the demands of Joe to "show your feelings" and "quit hiding behind your mask."

Anomics and groups

The anomic personality, who usually has a "weak" personality of social behavior, has special trouble in these groups. Maxine was easily victimized by Joe, who shone splendidly, dominating the group in the glory of his verbal presentation of himself. His own revelations were artificial. Joe was as out of touch with his real feelings as everyone else. He was trapped, too, and said so. Maxine felt frightened and guilty because she couldn't "get with it."

Now, some strong emotional responses were generated in this group. Both Maxine and Joe felt something had occurred by the end of the session. Something did occur. Individuals in the group interacted with one another through their personalities, their artificial reproductions of themselves. The emotions generated in that session decayed very quickly and joined all the other unfinished emotional situations that plagued both Maxine and Joe.

As indicated earlier, my own research with persons in these small groups has led me to believe that what happens or can happen in your own gestalt groups, as contrasted with what occurs in the artificial kind, should be given special attention. There is strong evidence (to be offered later) that there is an existing body of knowledge on how people may come together in small groups and find personal integration and self-awareness, and that individuals *can learn and use* this knowledge successfully.

Are you out of touch with yourself?

For now, consider a method for discovering if you have created an anomic or verbal personality for yourself. These are steps in a sequence or cycle that may occur quickly or over a period of days or weeks. They are clues, warnings that you are out of touch with yourself:

1. Prolonged boredom or apathy with yourself or others around you.
2. A kind of deadness of feeling, or detachment from what's going on around you.
3. A feeling of aimlessness in life, perhaps a halfhearted search for new things to do.
4. The stuck point; impasse.

The above can become a vicious circle, from boredom to impasse and back again. Both the verbal and anomic personality suffer in what I call the *stuck point*. They are stuck and can't break through to discover how they feel or to find new possibilities for themselves. The stuck point is a painful, punishing state to be in.

If you tend to live within your personality, you suffer an "ideal" gap: the conflict is between what you are and what you want to be. If you have created an anomic or verbal personality for yourself, you are wasting your energy in unnecessary conflict.

Again, most persons seem to be born with tendencies to become either over- or under-integrated in their social behavior. Far too few appear to be born with the ability to live as fully integrated persons without *learning* how to integrate their natural and social behaviors. If you are an under-integrated person, you have probably created an anomic personality for yourself. Or, if you are over-integrated, you have probably created a verbal personality for yourself.

You created your personality and you can change it to fit your human needs: someone to love who loves you in return; close friends; and work or activity that fits your own way of doing things.

Why does the myth of personality persist—this myth that insists you can adjust yourself to fit your personality, and that you *should* become this "well-adjusted" social robot? There are many, many reasons, but let me name a few that warrant special consideration at this point. First, there is a misunderstanding of human behavior. For too many years conventional psychology has accepted the view presented by the Freudians and Behaviorists that your personality is the real you.

Both of these schools of thought on human behavior maintain that your personality is the result of events beyond your control or power to change. The Freudians maintain that your conflicts with your parents and sisters or brothers molded you, and that you are a product of these conflicts.

The Behaviorist view

The Behaviorists differ, but the results are the same: You are molded from birth by external events which shape you, and it is beyond your power to change yourself. In either view, you are a powerless lump of clay, battered by circumstances, and it is beyond your ability to change. This gloomy philosophy is at the heart of the personality myth and provides the teeth for the personality trap.

There is another and perhaps more significant explanation of how this myth is maintained: The myth supports the personal wealth and social prestige of psychologists, psychiatrists, and those in related professions everywhere.

The established psychologist or psychiatrist, working in private practice, needs only eight to ten patients a week in psychotherapy to live well. All he needs is a few persons paying from $35 to $50 an hour to enjoy a lucrative weekly income, with little overhead expense. Many psychologists and other professionals supporting this myth work within institutions or for firms where they receive similar economic rewards.

Therapy is big business

The myth of personality is big business and pays well. The rewards are many—for therapists, most of whom seem to want to maintain their portion of the "personality myth": If you, as a person, do not know how you got the way you are, or how to change if you are in trouble, you need the professional to lead you out of the wilderness! So why disturb a profitable arrangement? Those who benefit from the arrangement— the therapists—are content.

Traditional therapists are wary of changes that threaten the myth that supports their financial gain and social prestige. But there is a far more serious issue at stake here than mere wealth and position: Traditional therapy invites a person to be sick as part of the therapeutic encounter. The person must play a "patient role" to get "treatment." Let there be no misunderstanding of this role. If you do not play the role, you will not be accepted for treatment, and if you can't pay for this drama, you won't get in the door.

The irony extends deeper. Many persons become ill trying to cram themselves into role expectations. This is what is wrong with them when they go to the therapist. Then, in conventional therapy, the "treatment" consists of inducing the person to adjust himself to roles in which he became "sick" in the first place.

Therapy can be a painful part of personality trap. Mental health care is already out of financial reach of most who need help. Well-established estimates within the professions are that one out of every four persons will need direct mental care sometime during his life. And, that over fifty percent of our hospital beds are occupied by persons suffering primarily from mental problems rather than physical illnesses.

One of my deeper concerns is the increasing use of drugs to "flatten out" the emotional reactions of persons in great pain because they are unable to adjust to fit some personality role. It is a fundamental mistreatment to use drugs to "flatten out," or quiet, the protesting, natural responses to pain in order to reestablish failed role behavior. Persons who use drugs to avoid this pain are increasing in number, and we put them in jail if they get caught using their drugs without a prescription. My belief is that the *legal abuse* of drugs is a greater danger, and is partly responsible for most of the *illegal* drug use.

It appears most urgent to find ways to teach the average person, who may be suffering greatly in this day-to-day struggle for good mental health, *how to avoid therapy and the personality trap*. The first step is to learn how to become a self-regulating person and this involves finding the real you. How this may be done is discussed in the following chapters.

2

The Anomic Personality

Geraldine—Jerry for short—is a prime example of an anomic personality. Jerry, a young woman of nineteen was pretty but tended to be overweight in spite of her many exotic diet plans. Weight was a source of daily worry for her. She didn't think she was attractive and constantly criticized her features and body.

Jerry had clusters of apprehensions about herself. This anxiety was expressed as fear and feelings of guilt. First, her parents had more or less disowned her. She was not close to either her father or mother. They seemed to prefer her older sister and younger brother.

Jerry was disorganized about herself, whether it was getting dressed, keeping her clothes up, helping around the house, keeping appointments, or adjusting to any routine. She was hard to live with. She lied, stole, and cheated in both little and big ways, but mostly in the small matters of everyday life. On the other hand, Jerry was affectionate, warm, loving, and deeply sympathetic toward others. She was good with children and animals. But her family and friends could barely put up with her disorganization.

Jerry couldn't stand herself. She toyed with the idea of suicide. That is, one time she sat with her legs dangling out the window of a two-story apartment building. She bought and carried pills to put herself to sleep permanently, maybe. She used marijuana, but not very much, perhaps once or twice. Actually, she was afraid to kill or hurt herself, even a little bit.

Jerry was convinced she was a lesbian. The only way she had experienced an orgasm was through oral sex. She liked it so much better than what she called "straight sex." But she was confused about why she didn't like to be around women. She didn't like women, and her sexual experiences had all been with men. Still, she found "straight sex" with a male painful. She believed there were two kinds of orgasm, clitoral and vaginal, and that she was capable only of the "clitoral orgasm." This was just one of many myths she believed. She masturbated regularly, and harshly criticized herself for not being able to stop.

Another problem for Jerry was her love affair with Robert, another anomic personality. Robert said he loved her, but she doubted him because he wouldn't change in certain ways that she felt would make her happy. She vacillated from moment to moment, and day to day, fretting over Robert's love or lack of love, whether he did or didn't. Robert seemed to care more for a boyfriend than he did for her. All three shared an apartment, a trio embroiled in conflict. The third party, Max, was a verbal personality, and he ruled the roost.

Jerry didn't have a single stable relationship with her family, lovers, or friends. She felt her life was a disaster, utterly beyond her power to correct. Her family forced her to move out, her lover tried to force her out of the apartment, and she was suspected of stealing at her salesclerk job and faced dismissal.

The extreme anomic personality is seen in the modern world as a misfit gumming up the works. In a world of technical organization, Jerry was slightly out of focus, disorganized and off-center, lost among men and machines. The anomic, in this view, is at best an awkward fit in a role-bound culture.

Jerry had a "weak" role pattern, a lack of roles in social behavior, and suffered confusion over roles to begin with. She didn't seem to know who or what she really was.

Anomics outnumber verbals

There are more anomic personalities than any other type. The anomic outnumbers the verbal by at least three or four to one. In other words, about seventy percent of the population tends to have an anomic personality. As an individual, the anomic personality may suffer great pain. The key to Jerry's problem involved both what she did with herself and what she did with others. Let's examine first what she did with herself.

Jerry was born with biological abilities which tended to make her an under-integrated person. This was her natural tendency. The personality she developed, the roles she adopted for herself, was an anomic personality. The under-integrated person with an anomic personality tends to respond too soon to feelings, that is, before his feelings have grown into an emotional response that integrates and organizes behavior.

For example, when Jerry met a person, say a young man, and she felt a sexual attraction, she responded too quickly to it. She responded before she noticed what all her other feelings about this man might be. Jerry criticized herself for always "picking losers." If she waited until she had more information about her other feelings, she might not attempt to establish a deep personal relationship with a "loser."

If Jerry could learn to wait for a range of feelings to a-rise, she might discover that although she feels that the man is sexually attractive, she also senses (feels) he is not very trustworthy, and could not be depended on to give her a sense of security or protection. Jerry wanted love which included not just sexual attraction, but bonds of affection, protection and security *within* an emotion of love.

Feelings are the beginning of emotion. Jerry responded at her feeling level, which disturbed and interfered with the emergence of her feelings and their growth into an emotional response. She did not allow a finished emotional response. Consequently, she did not know whether she was in love with anyone or not. In fact, Jerry didn't know how to recognize love, as she had never experienced its emotion. To summarize, Jerry had never experienced love because she had always responded too quickly to her feelings, blocking their growth into an emotional reaction.

The importance of emotional responses

A person must experience a completed emotional response because this response *integrates past experiences with present experience*. Feelings, the beginning of emotions, do not integrate one's past with the present situation. A person must have an emotional response in order to have a felt experience.

For example, when Jerry entered into a new situation in which she met someone for the first time, she was uneasy and a little frightened. These were her feelings. If Jerry could have waited and let her feelings grow, that is, if she could have accepted these beginnings of fear and uneasiness, and let them "build out" of the situation for a while, she would have had time to discover how she was organizing her past experiences from memory to meet the present situation.

The moment she met a stranger, all her past experience with new people attempted to be integrated with the present situation. If she waited until her past experiences combined and merged with the present (this happens very quickly), she might have found that it was natural for her to be cautious with strangers, and she didn't need to fear them until she had more "information" from her feelings. A feeling of fear might be discounted moments later by feelings of warmth and intellectual attraction.

By reacting at the feeling level, she experienced yet one more unfinished emotional response, which joined all the accumulation of unfinished emotions. It was a vicious circle and seriously alienating for Jerry. She stayed out of touch with herself and frequently found herself crying for no apparent reason. The "reason" is obvious: The crying was a way to relieve the pressure of all her unfinished emotional responses. *Crying* was an emotional response to the constant low-grade emergency in which she lived.

Thinking and acting in the present

There were several things Jerry needed to do, but the central effort began with very simple steps. She had to learn to *think and act in the present,* and ignore or overlook her first rise of feelings. This would be hard work but the steps were not difficult. She had to practice her regimen every day, very slowly at first, putting up with failures, and trying again when her efforts were unsuccessful.

First, she learned to make a decision that she could carry out completely within an hour or two at most. For instance, she wanted to get another job. Her decision was: "I will get another job. Today I will call the employment agency to make an appointment." The decision was to call the employment agency — which she could do at that moment. She decided and acted on her decision immediately.

She did not make a decision to get another job, and then say to herself, "I will go downtown tomorrow and look for another job." Her right decision was the one that permitted action to be taken at the time the decision was made. This is very important. Jerry had to learn to merge her thoughts and action in the present, that is, decide and act. Just little decisions at first until she got used to the combined act.

The combination of thinking and acting in the present began immediately to integrate Jerry's behavior and get her back in touch with herself. She experienced immediate results but it took much hard work and many months of practice before she could recognize the priority of her needs and act to gratify them.

But at first, she just made little decisions about minor matters that could be carried out without too much effort. Jerry practiced with these easy decisions until she became comfortable acting on thoughts at the time she had her "feelings." *To act with her feelings would allow her to experience an emotional response.* Her behavior would be a felt experience, and not end as an unfinished emotional situation.

There is another area in which Jerry worked with herself. She and her relatives did not understand what had happened to them as a family. In the early years, when parents and children were much younger, the family was a warm, affectionate, natural gestalt group. As children and parents grew older, this natural family group changed into an *artificial group*. The change occurred when the parents gradually shifted their emphasis from care of young children to the development of "well-adjusted personalities," with love and affection taking second place.

The shift from natural family group to artificial group

The shift from a natural gestalt group to an artificial social group, which transmitted the roles of personality formation, required that the family members interact with one another within their role personalities and not as individuals who cared for one another, regardless of the roles they played as mother, father, sister, or brother. This shift from a natural to an artificial emphasis is subtle and devastating, and fairly common in the urban world. Unfortunately, Jerry's parents, in their roles as mother and father, were satisfied with their children developing the "adjusted personalities" as "sons" or "daughters." Jerry interpreted this as meaning that her parents' preferred her sister or brother to her. Other family members made similar misinterpretations.

Jerry had great difficulty understanding why her parents, brother, and sister didn't seem to love her. She wanted them to accept her as she was, despite her inadequate personality of roles. The family members probably loved Jerry, but love was secondary to their primary emphasis on developing a good, "well-adjusted personality." This goal had been adopted by the entire family, Jerry included.

Jerry's brother and sister got more direct support from the parents because they developed the "right" personality. Jerry's main family role was one of "dependent child" of about ten years old. Her only other role was "artistic young woman struggling to be understood by the world," in conflict with "society." Neither of these roles was accepted by the other members of her family. Jerry had to learn that it was time to go outside the family to find her own natural gestalt groups, in which the primary reason for being together was to build bonds of personal care, love, recognition or individual attention outside the social behavior of individuals.

Misunderstanding of the revolution that families undergo is common and painful. Much of the time this shift from natural to artificial family group is not understood by any of the family members. That this is becoming increasingly common seems clear from several indications, not just from the disaffection of young persons from their families, but also from the spin-off of the elderly person from the average family. Both the young and the elderly are seeking a separate affectional base outside the social family group. As will be seen later, this shift from being a natural group to being an artificial group by families is part of the reason for the widespread popularity of the encounter or sensitivity group phenomenon.

Two areas need attention

Jerry's problems, then, needed attention in two different directions: practice in thinking and acting in the present; and establishment of new, personal gestalt groups of her own, where her "personality" was secondary to her friendship or love. This was a difficult task but was very rewarding for her. Sometime in her life, Jerry might be able to return to her family group with a stronger, more acceptable role structure, as a "new personality," and have relationships there again. If this occurs, she won't be asking her family to adjust their personalities to fit hers—and they may then interact somewhat more comfortably in their family roles.

Let us examine another anomic "personality," this time a male of thirty-five. Let's call him Harold. Harold was married and worked as a typesetter in a printing firm. He was tagged by most of those who knew him as a "born loser." He was a pleasant person who was stepped on by everyone.

Harold's "personality"

Harold had great difficulty in expressing himself verbally. He had a mild stutter and usually said nothing of meaning when he did speak. Though able to write much better than he could talk, he hadn't anyone to write to. He had a gentle smile, was unassuming, and blended into the background wherever he was. It took him a long time to become efficient at his job, and he had trouble with any innovation in his work or in his private life.

Harold couldn't read road maps; he didn't have a good sense of space and direction, such as north and south; and he forgot numbers, dates, appointments, names, and faces. He had to work very hard to organize himself and generally he let others do this for him. He wanted them to. He resented being the way he was and silently blamed those who "organized" him.

In short, other persons took care of Harold. He was "sweet" and seemed appreciative, and really enjoyed being around others. He couldn't stand to be alone, even for a few hours. He seemed to trap others neatly with his personality. Most of those close to him soon discovered they were bound in a tight grip.

Harold was "sensitive" and easily hurt. Those around him, once they had taken the responsibility for his "feelings," realized there was an intricate pattern of care involved. They found they had to adjust themselves quite a bit to Harold. He didn't like dirty jokes; he was uncomfortable with children; he didn't drink; he wanted special foods; he slept lightly; he had many different aches and pains; and he had virtually no sex life. A major problem was that Harold's wife, Christine, felt she nearly "raped" him on occasion, that he lacked aggressive physical love for her. She disliked the elaborate ritual necessary for him to get "ready." She wanted him to get her "ready" now and then.

As muddled and fussy as Harold appeared to his family and friends, the problems described were minor, in his view, compared to his state of terror. His inner, secret life was filled with unpleasant memories, and his sleep was disturbed by nightmares. He was unable to talk about his terror, and even those close to him were unaware of how much pain he experienced. They knew he was a worrywart, but they believed they had adjusted to this and accepted his sensitivity of feelings. Inasmuch as Harold's family, friends, and fellow workers had put up with him and his conditions for years, it was no wonder they didn't like him very much.

Harold was so out of touch with himself, he wasn't sure how to express how he felt. As with Jerry in the earlier example, Harold responded too quickly to his feelings and disturbed the emergence of an emotional reaction. He didn't know how he felt down deep. If someone asked him, he waited until he thought he knew what the other person was feeling, then he'd say he was feeling that way too; or, he might just say, "I don't know."

Remedial efforts begin by finishing emotional situations

How does one help Harold? Rather, how does he help himself? Harold's central effort began with working through his unpleasant memories and the nightmares of his sleep. This was hard work, but he gained immediately in his efforts. Unpleasant memories are unfinished emotional situations. Dreams also are unfinished emotional situations. Nightmares are vivid, strong, unfinished emotional responses. Once Harold had worked through each unpleasant memory and nightmare, they vanished. There is nothing mysterious about unpleasant memories or dreams, in spite of conventional myths to the contrary. However, it is difficult and takes a great deal of effort for a person to work them through.

Unfinished emotional situations always surround a need that has not been gratified—love, sex, attention, approval, protection, and so on. It may be a minor need; but in order for memories or dreams to continue, generally one of the more basic needs is involved. Only Harold could work this through. He didn't need an expert, for Harold really was the only expert on his memories.

Resentment—a product of anxiety

By being an anomic personality and responding too soon to his inner and outer experiences, Harold had accumulated a growing pile of unfinished emotional responses and un-gratified needs. He lived in a state of low-grade emergency of emotion, or anxiety. This anxiety was expressed as fears and guilt feelings, which finally caused him to resent nearly everyone around him, as if they were responsible somehow for his predicament.

Pleasant memories of past experiences fade into the background and are only recalled when they are being integrated into the whole of a new experience. This is the healthy dynamic. But unpleasant memories hang around as part of the low-grade emotional emergency that alienates a person and keeps him out of touch with himself.

The following describes how Harold learned to work through his unpleasant memories and nightmares. Harold found periods of time when he could be by himself. At first he needed real solitude, until he got accustomed to how his therapy worked.

Sitting by himself in the quiet of his room, Harold deliberately recalled his strongest unpleasant memory and re-created it *as if it were happening at the moment*. This was crucial. If he didn't recapture the memory as if it were occurring at the moment, he couldn't work it through. He had to pretend that the event or circumstance was happening as he first experienced it, that it was happening *at that moment*.

He tried to recapture every detail. Where were the events happening? In a street or building? In an open field? What was going on? A conversation – a fight – what? Who was in the scene? How were they dressed? Were there sounds or odors? What were the colors? Was it night or day? It was often necessary for him to repeat the image several times, much as television does with "instant replay" of sports events.

The unfinished emotions surrounding unpleasant memories or dreams are revealed only after extensive, detailed examination of what was being dreamed or imagined. There may be layers of feelings concealing the unfinished emotional response. Harold got sweaty and fearful, and stopped his efforts many times before he learned how to push on through the many feelings that surrounded a deeper emotion. He worked through one nightmare after about three weeks effort. Another he resolved in one try.

The one that took three weeks to work through gave him more insight about himself than any experience he had ever had. He kept working at it in spite of his feeling of repulsion towards a particularly grotesque animal that seemed to want to give him a slobbery physical embrace. Underneath this bizarre creature's exterior repulsiveness, Harold found a simple ungratified need: He had never felt he could love anyone and that someone could love him. This insight came very suddenly, after much effort – and he was done with the nightmare. Harold worked through several unpleasant memories and discovered connections not only with the nightmare, but also with other ungratified areas in his life. Even his sex life began to change, to the delight of his wife.

But there were crises, too. Harold concluded that his job was unbearable. He had always wanted to "do something creative" with other persons. After two or three false starts in different occupations, he attended a hair-styling school and found a "fit." He struggled hard with this discovery. For the first time in his life he enjoyed "working" at something, and didn't view it as toil. He felt creative and positive. But he had to battle with his disapproval of hair styling as an occupation for a man.

Harold didn't care for male company. He was not homosexual or effeminate. He liked women, and wanted to be around them rather than men. He had always felt that preference, but worried and had guilt feelings about it.

The hair-styling job was a real boon for Harold. He related better to living things than to objects. He liked to be physically close to people, to touch them. In his old typesetter's job, he worked directly with a machine, a thing, an object, and he hated it. And his life as well. In his new hairstyling job, he could work with persons he preferred – women – and be in close touch with them as part of his duties. He found a creative fit for himself after a few months of deliberate search.

A third anomic personality: June

In another example of the anomic personality, a quite different problem appears. Let's call this woman June. June was thirty-two, and had only two roles which she tended to use for all situations. When she wasn't acting in one of her roles, she was unable to talk about herself or about anything. She remained silent.

June's two roles were: a child of eight or nine; and a bright, liberal college student struggling to become successful and wealthy. She had different voices for each role. In the child role, her voice was a soft, whiny monotone, which she used in a quarrelsome, pleading, childlike manner.

In her bright-liberal-college-student role, her voice sharpened, hardened and became clipped; her manner was positive and assertive. June could talk with machine-gun speed in that role.

Her major problems, as she saw them, were that she couldn't feel sexual intercourse and that she became hysterical halfway through the act (or sooner). She generally ended up crying or nauseated. June was warm and loving, and needed and wanted to be touched; thus, her reaction to the sexual act terrified her. She imagined herself to be insane. June *lived in the future.* She attempted to anticipate the future, and let that imagined future determine the present.

Let's illustrate her problem with an actual example. June was cleaning her apartment. She planned beforehand to do the living room first, then the kitchen, then the bedroom, and last of all, the bathroom. While she was cleaning the living room, she was thinking about cleaning the kitchen; while cleaning the kitchen, she thought about cleaning the bedroom; then, while cleaning the bedroom, she was thinking about the bathroom. Always, even though "organized," she attempted to exist one step ahead of herself in the future. The present, the actual cleaning of each room, was inadequately experienced.

The result was that she cleaned haphazardly, and had to go back time and again to do things she "forgot" or "didn't see" while cleaning. She did a bad job because she was living in the next room, a place where she never would be! She was out of touch with her present experience, and this was maddening. She could not understand why she did everything so badly, whether cooking, cleaning, studying, talking with someone, or having sexual intercourse.

During a sexual experience, even at the moment when her partner entered her body, June was imagining how she might feel *after* the experience, or, how it might feel to have an orgasm. She never let herself feel the experience at the moment it was actually happening.

Responding too soon is typically anomic

This responding too soon to feelings that have not yet occurred is typically anomic. June had never experienced the sexual emotions that would lead to orgasmic response. Feelings are the beginning of emotions, but June attempted to anticipate her feelings, to be just one step in the future. She was always just ahead of herself, worrying, fretting about how things are or should be, blaming herself when they didn't occur.

People like June appear to be ripe for a psychotherapist. But June, like our other subjects, managed to align her feelings with events as they happen, without spending time on the couch. The major effort for June was to begin to practice feeling herself in the present. A change in her responses could occur if she "practiced" feeling what was happening to her, and stopped anticipating what might happen later. This meant that, to change June's responses to intercourse, her partner had to proceed slowly and, at times, do nothing until June had time to feel the experience. She had to learn to wait until she could identify where the sensation was and how it felt.

"Feeling" is important

Practice for June consisted of thinking about what was happening to parts of her body, such as her vagina, thinking that they really existed as part of her. As silly as it might sound, June finally took a hand mirror and looked at herself, and for the first time in her life, examined what she could see of her sexually responsive body areas. This action, plus some "clinical" practice sessions with her partner, where she deliberately started intercourse and stopped when she didn't feel sensations, produced gains within two or three weeks. By then, she had begun to enjoy her sex activity, and by not pushing herself, was able to learn how to respond with full sexual emotion. Her main guidelines were: Don't continue if you lose feeling at any time. Stop, slow down, return to the beginning and start over – until feeling returns – or quit, and try again some other time. Do just those things that produce feeling.

There was another area of major importance for June. And she worked through it during the period of getting in touch with sex feelings. She threw away most of her clothes and keepsakes!

June's closets and rooms were filled with things she really didn't like. (Anomics tend not to relate well to objects or things. They have trouble if they try to have emotional attachments that "go against the grain.") She had very few dresses, skirts, underclothes, shoes, or any other objects that she cared about.

This is disastrous for an anomic, and bad gestalt for any-one. Every time June put on something that she didn't like, she created an unfinished emotional situation. She wore things because she had bought them, and didn't want to throw them out because she was thrifty.

June had to learn *not* to wear clothes she didn't like. It was *very* hard for her to do, but she did it. She went through every closet and drawer and found that there was hardly an item in them she really cared for—among all the things she wore or was keeping to wear at some time "in the future."

I remember the analogy of the woman with a beachball in a pool. She spends most of her energy holding the beach-ball under the surface. To live in the future, June had to keep both hands on the beachball of her present unfinished emotions to keep them under water, under control. Her life was filled with one beachball after another, one unfinished situation after another. Day after day, more and more energy was needed to keep her beachball submerged.

The debris of unfinished business

June's clothes, mementos, bric-a-brac, and other objects held little meaning for her. So, she systematically went through her belongings and tossed out her "beachball," all the unfinished debris of her life that cluttered her existence with meaninglessness. She didn't keep a thing she didn't have some feeling for, and couldn't use in the present. Out went her clothes, except for the few items she liked. She went out and bought others that fit her emotionally and physically. She threw away dozens of books that she kept to read in "the future."

June hoarded junk in the way a squirrel hoards nuts, but the junk never "fed" her. Everything she kept that she didn't like or find useful became another "beachball," part of the debris of unfinished business. More than anything else, it was this cleaning out of things which she had no feeling for that probably got June started toward full emotional health. It cleared the decks for getting in touch with herself.

Some persons who tend to be under-integrated do not create such visible anomic personalities as illustrated in the examples above. But these "invisible" anomics far out-number all the other under-integrated persons. Invisible anomics are partially integrated in some ways but live a life filled with disappointment with themselves. A weak role pattern and basic disorganization plague their lives.

An "invisible" anomic

Jack, an interesting man of forty, is a good example. People usually are "crazy" about Jack. Jack cares about others, is generous (too generous, some say), kind, and thoroughly enjoys doing things with his many friends. He is a social gadabout, always on the go, always ready to include strangers as well as friends in his many projects.

Jack is liked wherever he goes and is described as "old easy going Jack, a real fun guy." Failed plans and disasters don't seem to bother him. He laughs them off and helps others feel better when things go wrong. He has only good things to say about others, too.

Employers like Jack. His wife, Margaret, thinks he is "about the cutest thing alive," most of the time. Margaret is an under-integrated person, but has a more anomic person-ality than her husband Jack. She doesn't talk much and is happy only when Jack is around. He takes her everywhere he goes. They get along well together, enjoy each other, and have a good sex life. Margaret is like Claudia, the fictional character described in Rose Franklyn's novel of that title: lovable, well-meaning, moody, unpredictable, childlike and dependent.

Margaret and Jack have to work very hard, underneath it all, to hold their world together. These two anomics lean on one another for mutual support—lest a strong wind blow both of them away. They are good parents and love their children. But their children have been reared from birth largely by their grandparents. The children don't mind, and thrive on having three homes to shuttle among.

Jack has only one role and he uses it as his whole personality: He plays the *friend* role, his basic integrating role. Jack is a friend to his wife, his children, his boss, his coworkers, and to strangers. He also could be a husband, a father, and a lover, but for all those roles he substitutes his friend role because it is the only one he has learned to adjust himself to. Much of Jack's genuine behavior fits the friend role and most persons are not aware of how hard he works at it.

The "friend" role in marriage

Jack is primarily a friend to his wife, and she adjusts herself to fit this friend role too. They are good friends first, and only secondarily are husband and wife, father and mother. Now, this condition is sensed not only by Jack and Margaret, but also by their parents, children, friends, and coworkers. All have some uneasiness, albeit minor, about Jack and Margaret, as do they themselves. With Jack and Margaret, the uneasiness has settled into occasional fear and guilt, which they don't understand. Despite the problems, this anomic couple may survive and enjoy a much better than average life. But there are perils.

Jack and Margaret have several natural gestalt groups in which they have love, care, protection, and personal identity. The couple are one gestalt group, and, with their children, they have a family gestalt.

Jack has to work hard each day to stay organized. He enjoys his job, but his hidden efforts are great. He occasionally commits a major blunder, such as leaving out a crucial cost estimate in an advertising plan. He tries to anticipate where he will blunder, but he spends too much time on staying organized in the routine affairs of his life.

Jack maintains a rigid daily calendar to guide himself. This works some of the time, but it takes him months to change to a new way of doing things. He has to work many extra hours to learn new techniques, or to develop new habits. This bothers him, and he is silently very critical of himself. Jack works very hard just to stay even with others who, it seems to Jack, are so much better organized without the effort Jack makes.

There are other areas in which Jack "controls" himself. He coasts along with only one or two drinks on social occasions, for he knows he can't handle liquor. He gets drunk on two or three drinks, unless they are spaced over several hours. Jack loses money, and leaves hats, coats, and other things everywhere. Neither Jack nor Margaret relate to objects well and their home is one cluttered room after another. He buys two or three of everything, hoping that he will be able to find at least one when he needs it. Food, pens, clothes, or what have you—he buys "sets" of things and strategically places them around where he can find them.

Each pair of grandparents are another gestalt group for them, and they have three or four friendship groups of coworkers and outside friends that are natural gestalts, where the members care for one another outside their personality of roles. As long as Jack and Margaret have this wealth of natural gestalt groups they can hardly go wrong. It is the stuff of life. The hazards come when these supporting gestalt groups spin off and are not replaced. The pattern is familiar.

The children grow older and leave, perhaps move out of town. Jack and Margaret's parents will die eventually. Friends and coworkers come and go in the usual course of events. Unless these gestalt groups are renewed as the years pass—and filled in with other groups—Jack and Margaret will have a tough time. And they probably won't know what is happening to them because they can't see it coming.

The above is not an unusual example. It happens all the time.

A review of the characteristics of the anomic personality

Let me review the various characteristics of the anomic personality revealed in the examples in this chapter. These are general characteristics, common to most persons who have created anomic personalities for themselves. As shown by the examples, some anomics have more problems with one or two traits than with the whole range of flaws that plague an under-integrated person.

But usually, all the anomic patterns are present in varying degrees. When any one of these anomic behavior traits is integrated into a person's natural behavior, it tends to stimulate integration of the other anomic difficulties. Natural and social behavior are both parts of a whole. Change one and the other is involved in change. Any part of a person's behavior that becomes integrated has a positive influence on the rest of the person's behavior.

The anomic is deficient in roles

Being too roleless, the anomic tends *to respond too soon* to feelings before an emotional response has had time to emerge. Anxiety always results from an unfinished emotional response. *The anxiety in the anomic flows into emotions of fear and guilt.*

The anomic has difficulty in recognizing the *priority of needs,* since needs get mixed up in the disturbed flow of feelings. He confuses needs, sex, hunger, love, and so on, since feelings do not build into an emotional response that organizes behavior to answer a need. He has too many feelings, not enough emotion.

The anomic tends to *live in the future.* In attempting to live in the future, just a step or two ahead of himself, he blocks the natural process of behavior that integrates past experiences into the present moment. He fears the future. This futuristic pattern *prevents the anomic from having felt experiences* in the present. A felt experience involves an emotional response that integrates past experiences with the present moment. The anomic largely has *unfelt experiences.* He fears the future because he does not have felt experiences in the present.

The anomic has trouble thinking and acting in the present. He has a *poor memory.* The anomic has trouble integrating past experience with the present because he is trying to live in the future. Memory is the integration of the past with present experience and he doesn't allow this merging to happen.

The anomic tends to play an underdog role to someone else's topdog. He *tends to be submissive* and lets others take responsibility for his behavior. The anomic is not self-regulating and prefers some external controls for behavior.

The anomic does not have much of *a sense of passage of time*, or of space and direction, or where things — including himself — exist in space. He has little sense of space or time boundaries, where they begin and end. He frequently feels he is part of a world without boundaries, like a drop of water becoming part of a lake.

The anomic is *plagued by unpleasant memories* surrounding unresolved emotional experiences. Unpleasant dreams are also common. He generally *lacks verbal ability* to express himself.

The anomic *relates better to persons than to objects or things. He does not make good contact* with objects — he does not understand too well *how things fit together* in machines. He may be afraid to scrub a surface hard enough to clean it, or to turn a nut tightly enough on a bolt.

The anomic does not have *a feel for his body,* an awareness that it is all together. He may lack body grace or a sense of muscle tone.

The anomic is out of touch with himself. He doesn't taste food adequately, or hear, see, or feel through his senses fully since he makes such poor contact with the outer world. The anomic may appear to be a disaster. But in some ways he is the more human of the personality types, including the integrated person. But the anomic is too human, if that makes sense!

A similarity between anomics and verbals

A major similarity between the anomic and verbal personality should be noted before we move on. Both may "experience" themselves as having split or dual personalities —

a sense of having a Dr. Jekyll and Mr. Hyde type of struggle. This awareness may be a source of major alienation within themselves. As noted earlier, this is a sign of recognition of the distance between their natural and their social behavior, the lack of being an integrated person.

We shall return to the anomic, but let us now go on to the next chapter, a study of verbal personalities.

3

The Verbal Personality

Tom was a man of forty who had risen nearly to the top of his profession in business management. He operated his home and managed his personal affairs with the same spit-and-polish efficiency that characterized his office work. Let's follow him on an average day.

Tom had a verbal personality. He got up every morning at the same time, even on weekends and holidays. He had trained himself to awaken without an alarm and he was proud of it. He greeted each morning with this role of self-control, of "the healthy person getting up on time." Those who lived with Tom had adjusted to this role. That is, everyone in the family had adopted the healthy-person-gets-up-early role.

Tom's wife and children were organized around his many roles, his personality of social behavior. He used the bathroom first, his breakfast was prepared and waiting for him at a set time, and he was always there ready to eat. His food was cooked a certain way. His eggs had to be boiled to a certain hardness or he wouldn't eat them. But his wife, Betty, had learned to cook the eggs just right and only occasionally did she have to do them over.

Tom was neat, clean, and a very well-organized person. Betty arranged his clothes meticulously, placing them in special spots, in neat stacks, or on hangers, precisely where he wanted them to be.

When Tom got up, he bathed, ate, dressed, and left for work on schedule. His timing was accurate enough to set a watch by. At the office, the role routine continued. Tom had a neat, expert secretary. He tried about a dozen anomics before he found a verbal type who could adjust herself to fit his style and his roles.

Tom was very good at his job as a management consultant and efficiency expert in cost analysis and personnel organization. He had pleasant manners and spoke so softly that others had to strain to hear him. He had a gentle smile with a disarming little chuckle that bubbled up when he made a point others didn't quite understand.

I am sure you recognize other verbal personalities like Tom, for they are pervasive. You find them in industry, science, education and politics—wherever there's a need for a "take-over" person. They are the most sought-after persons in our society. The computer-age culture lies at their feet.

Other persons didn't care much for Tom. His wife Betty, his children, his boss, his coworkers, all the persons who came in contact with him, didn't like him as a person. They often described their feelings about him by saying they "admired and respected" him, and that he was a "fine" man and "very dependable." But hardly anyone would talk to Tom about personal matters—only strangers might—until they got to know him.

For that matter, Tom didn't care too much for himself either. He believed his feelings and emotions were a weakness that he had to control. When a strong feeling crept up past his self-control, he quickly pushed it down and turned his thoughts to more "objective" things. And he expected others to do the same. Feelings were for women and children, not men, he believed.

Tom was over-integrated into social behavior, with too much "personality." Where the anomic personality suffers anxiety expressed as fears and guilt feelings, the verbal personality suffers anxiety expressed in violence. This aggression, this violence, may be directed toward the individual, toward others, or toward objects. Verbals probably number less than twenty percent of the population but account for most of the violence. The verbal personality is exposed usually by his talk. Whether spoken talk or written talk, he brims with talk-talk and talk about talk. But for the verbal personality, this talk-talk is not "felt" talk; it is unfelt experience and he is in pain.

Tom suffered, and his world suffered with him. He experienced a constant low-grade anxiety that he expressed by violence with words. Although soft-spoken, he punished those around him with words. As he was critical of himself, he punished himself with words too. But no one heard the silent, inner thoughts relating to his self-castigation.

Tom's family, neighbors, coworkers, and friends had all felt the sting, the sharp thrust, the attack and punishment of his words. He knew how to win an argument. Behind that soft voice was a punishing tyrant whose most common admonition was: "If I can do it, so can you!"

Tom's personality affected his family

His wife Betty was the loneliest woman on the block. She organized herself and the children the best she could to fit Tom's many role schedules. She spent great amounts of energy anticipating, preparing, and arranging things and persons to fit Tom's roles, the way he wanted himself and others to be. She suffered a great deal. She cried (but only when alone) and blamed herself for not being a "better wife," aware that something was radically wrong. She had three children, a "regular" sex life, "regular" weekends together, "regular" hobbies together, and "regular" plans for the future. But Betty and Tom seldom talked with one another outside their "regular" roles, their regulated life.

Tom could go through an entire evening at home and not say a word. Betty often attempted conversation, to discuss matters she thought might interest him, but it usually proved fruitless. She had given up long before trying to talk about herself and the things that filled her life, because they seemed so unimportant to her husband.

An anomic, Betty hadn't the slightest idea of how Tom felt about anything. His prolonged silences were nearly as punishing as his verbal attacks. Occasionally she would plead with him to try to understand why she failed in so many different ways as a wife. Meanwhile, Tom insisted that she seek help from a physician or psychiatrist. But Betty had done this and was too frightened to tell him that the family physician recommended they both go, together.

Tom was convinced that his wife needed "some pills to straighten out her emotions." Even when Tom silently noted that things were not all going well for him, he "talked himself out of it." He believed that although he suffered a wild surge of nearly uncontrollable feelings once in a while, basically he was sound and "right," and could get things under control, given time. He also contended that if he was not right in what he was doing, he was *more* right than most other persons who were not "objective" but allowed their emotions to rule their lives.

How Tom dealt with his problem

Tom had a lot of work to do with himself to integrate his natural and social behavior, and to relax the grip of his personality on his real self. Where the anomic responds too soon to feelings (the beginning of emotion), Tom stamped out, or suppressed, his feelings before they grew. Where the anomic tends to live in the future, Tom tended to live in the past. His roles were past bound, based upon how things were done yesterday, or last year, or by custom or tradition. Years ago, his father taught him that mistakes shouldn't have to be repeated and that he would never get ahead unless he organized himself every waking moment.

Tom had to learn how to quit suppressing his feelings. He did not experience the emotions of love, anger, hate, joy, sadness, and contentment. By blocking his feelings, these emotions did not occur, and he lived in a state of unfinished emotional emergency.

The first step for Tom was learning how to daydream. (He believed that only weak persons daydream; therefore he quit when he was young.) Tom was encouraged to devote a few minutes a day to deliberate daydreaming. This was difficult work for him.

The results of Tom's work

After several weeks, Tom underwent some marked changes. He learned to "let go" in his daydreams, and was astonished by their rich and wild content. They frightened him sometimes and he would stop for days, then return cautiously. At first his daydreams were filled with visions of power, enormous wealth, zooming cars and airplanes, speed, and swinging high and free above the earth. These were frightening to him, however, so he finally dreamed of other sorts of things.

The new daydreams or fantasies began as vague, unformed swirls and shapes that reflected inner thoughts. Slowly images popped into his daydreams—images of naked bodies, glimpses of men and women, genitals, breasts, and bare limbs. Also he envisioned persons having sex in a variety of ways.

Tom was encouraged to change his sex habits (roles) with his wife. Instead of assuming the "missionary position," and following his old routine, Tom let Betty be aggressive, and change their familiar interplay. This did not come about suddenly, but took several months. The process was speeded up when Betty deliberately plied Tom with a few extra martinis. He seldom drank more than one or two, and then only on weekends.

Tom and Betty had relaxed a little in their role-bound sex but one night Betty discarded all her caution. She brought Tom to sexual climax orally, then stimulated him again, orally, for "regular" intercourse. This was one of the most prolonged and satisfying sexual experiences either had had.

The daydreams that led to the change in sex roles were the beginning of Tom's learning what to do to relinquish his grip on himself, and thereby integrate his natural and social behavior. Still, it was just a beginning.

Contrast of an anomic and a verbal

Tom and Betty are good examples of the contrast between the verbal and anomic personalities. Where Tom had too many roles and too much personality, Betty had too few roles and too little personality. Betty, being more roleless, tended to adjust herself to fit Tom's roles, whatever they were. Sometimes these roles fitted Betty, but mostly not. For instance, Betty enjoyed cooking, and was delighted to "organize" herself around getting meals ready to accommodate Tom. But in most other areas, Tom's roles were difficult for Betty to adjust to, although she tried. She tried to be organized so that she could be ready to leave on time for social engagements or trips, but was forever behind while Tom paced, ready to leave.

In contrast to Betty, who responded too soon to her feelings, Tom didn't recognize his feelings when they occurred. Betty lost her appetite if the food looked too greasy, regardless of how it smelled or tasted. Tom ignored any of his reactions to the food, and cared only that it was prepared the way he wanted it and served on time.

Another major contrast was in their use of words in self-expression. Betty frequently couldn't find words to describe her emerging feelings. She didn't know how to link words to describe her inner feelings. Conversely, Tom used words well, but attempted to adjust himself to fit the words. He used words to replace feelings. For example, when Betty met someone for the first time, she was at a loss as to what to say, and mumbled some cliché. Tom always knew what to say on meeting a stranger. He had a role for that. He played the how-nice-to-meet-you role, and assumed that he shouldn't have any feelings about a stranger anyway. This is a major and typical difference between verbal and anomic personalities. The verbal uses words to replace his natural behavior, and combines the words within a role of adopted social manners or group ways of doing things.

Anomic Betty lived through the "personality" of roles of verbal Tom. It was a strange but common alliance and was an artificial existence for both—one responding too soon, the other not responding at all with genuine behavior. Betty daydreamed a lot, mostly about the future. She lived too much in her daydreams. Tom didn't daydream at all until he began experimenting with himself. Tom had a good "object" imagination (another difference between the anomic and verbal), especially concerning the relationship of objects to each other. Good at math, he could conjure complex problems and solve them "mentally." This was his sole creative expression.

He could spend hours mentally manipulating symbols, formulas, and "things" in their relationship to other things. But neither he nor other persons were ever part of this mental imagery—just objects and things, numbers, and written pages of facts or words. His mental imagery did not include living persons.

Also, Tom didn't have a sense of humor, and didn't know how to laugh. He missed the point of most jokes. Betty laughed a lot (except around Tom) and sometimes daydreamed about "funny" situations.

Integration begins

Integration for Tom started with the discovery of his sexual needs and unfinished emotions surrounding those needs. It took Tom some time to explore his daydreams, to change his sex roles, and to allow himself free sexual expression. He might come to discover he loved Betty if he could free his other suppressed feelings. Love is an emotion that grows from a variety of different feelings that have converged to produce it. Warmth, security, protection, stability—all these feelings are involved in an emotion of love.

Now, one role never stands alone. A role always involves a "cluster" of roles related to each other. When Tom abandoned his "missionary sex" role with Betty, he found other roles changed, too. He had never undressed in front of Betty, nor had he run around the house without a robe. He had never let her see him using the toilet. All of these ways of acting were roles. Tom discovered that Betty didn't mind climbing in the tub while he was bathing. In fact, he was shocked that Betty wanted to see him "in action." This violated his "privacy" roles.

Discovering the dominant need

Let's return to Tom's work with himself. He had to take each one of his major roles, with the cluster of roles related to that role, and work—through imagination and deliberate daydreaming—to discover the dominant need and accompanying emotion that were unresolved or unfinished. He had to work through each area in which he was at a "stuck point."

Tom started on his sex habits, which were roles. This was his most dominant unfinished need seeking resolution through full emotional response. Perhaps the next stuck point would be his food habits—all the roles surrounding the way he ate. It might be that his work roles would emerge as the most dominant unfinished situation. In other words, he must find his most pressing incomplete need, and seek resolution. This could be done by letting the free flow of his imagination shape his daydreams. He had to try not to *force* this to the surface of awareness, but rather to let the need emerge on its own, and take shape in his fantasy thoughts. This is the path to discovery if you are at a stuck point in life.

The most difficult discovery to make about deliberate fantasy, the use of daydreams, is to make certain you pretend the fantasy is occurring as if it were happening now, in the present. Anomic Betty tended to daydream of the future— tomorrow, or some vague time ahead. Tom's daydreaming tended toward fantasies in the past, about things that already had occurred. Effective use of healthy daydreaming requires that the fantasy be imagined in the present moment, as if it were happening here and now. This, I repeat, is one of the hardest tasks to learn. Futuristic or historical daydreaming, dreams of the future or past, only serve to reinforce the alienation of feelings.

Unfinished needs and emotions are always in the present, and will burst through the stuck point if the individual, by means of the fantasy, accepts their reality in the present. Tom had to learn that when one basic need and its accompanying emotion was unfinished, the emergence to his awareness of all his other needs was blocked.

Tom was well on his way to resolving his sexual needs. These would subside and get out of the way of his other pressing needs, as long as he continued to fulfill his sexual needs. They rose and fell, emerged and subsided as they were gratified.

As noted earlier, Tom may have found that his eating habits needed direct attention next. After he worked through these and discarded roles that didn't lead to his genuine gratification with food (he didn't experience much taste or smell of food), he could then work through his next problem, his "office" roles.

The priority of needs and their gratification

Tom, like all of us, had a priority of needs and unfulfilled emotional responses to them. The need for love, security, human warmth, excitement, and growth are all needs of the first order of priority. These needs do not occur at the same time. At any moment in time one will be more urgent than another and seek gratification. You get hungry (need food) and then you eat, and the need subsides until you get hungry again. If you don't eat, pretty soon your hunger for food will overwhelm your attention with its urgency. Most needs do not reach such clear intensity, of course. But Tom had several basic needs that he was not responding to because he had blocked the rise of emotions that organized him to act on those needs.

Tom's sexual needs were only partially fulfilled within his sex-habit roles. He never experienced the full emotional response of not only having sex but doing so with a person he wanted to love. This unfinished emotion surrounding his sexual needs had never been a *felt experience* until he changed what he was doing with himself.

Tom was shocked at the things he and Betty had done on that "big night." He had trouble "looking Betty in the face" for several days after. He was more shocked by Betty's behavior than by his enjoyment of what she did. The experience interfered with his efficiency on his job. There were unpleasant after effects. Once change like this is "pumped in," relationships are never the same again. But even with this knowledge, Tom recognized that he had gained far more than he had lost. He felt a stirring within, and began to feel alive for the first time in his life.

A description of Jean—a second verbal personality

Let's examine another verbal personality. Jean was thirty-two and had never been married. She was the top executive secretary in an advertising firm. Efficient, brilliant at her work, she could run the place virtually on her own. Her boss couldn't do without her. She had seen to that.

Jean willingly took on even the smallest responsibility and organized it to fit her way of doing things. She was admired, respected, and sought after by employers, but was feared by nearly everyone around her.

Jean had several male and female "friends." But there were rigid role requirements one had to meet to be in her favor. Her friends were expected to adjust themselves to "fit" Jean or she dropped them. They had to be on time, dress well, read the right things, and go to the right places or they were out. She allowed people to tell her where they wanted to go or what they wanted to do, but if they were so presumptuous as to disagree with what she wanted, she said nothing, but that was the end of the relationship.

A charming tyrant, Jean didn't talk much except when she was playing her basic role of organizing everyone's life around her. She would visit a house and change furniture around. She would straighten pictures on the wall, as they "drove her crazy" if crooked.

About the worst affront a friend could commit was to have an untidy bathroom. Jean said nothing if the bath was not spotless, but she didn't come back. Clean bathrooms were a compulsion with her. Most of her behavior was compulsive; it was as if she were driven to clean up the messy persons in the world.

Jean hated herself and others with nearly equal intensity. She hated to menstruate, hated to use the bathroom, disliked taking time to eat, and hated sex—even though she "clinically" attacked one of her male friends about once every six months. She had decided that this was enough for her needs.

Jean didn't have a single personal friend of any consequence. She had two or three female friends who weren't really close and who lived out of town. Jean wrote to them and got along much better by just writing. Once in a while, one of them would be in town and would meet Jean for lunch; then they would go their separate ways and perhaps meet again the following year. These out-of-towners were the only persons Jean considered close friends, and occasionally she felt sad (but shrugged it off) that all her good friends seemed always to be persons who had moved away. Jean ritually clung to these long-distance relationships long after the friends saw little reason to "keep in touch."

Jean had a brief, one-time homosexual experience with one of her friends. She dropped the friend abruptly, and never saw her again. Disgusted with herself, resenting her friend, her self-reproach turned to self-hate. Deep down Jean didn't feel she was homosexual, but she did feel she had betrayed herself.

This belief of self-betrayal led to more rigid self-controls. She quickly started having stomach trouble which grew into an ulcer. Although she managed to keep her ulcer under control, she had a hysterectomy, and then was able to say she had had her "female organs" removed. She insisted on a clean sweep and the surgeon obliged her.

Jean related best to objects

Jean was not an uncommon type of verbal personality. Her stuck point was that she related best to objects or things, and got along only with those persons whom she could treat as objects (things) too, including herself. Jean had a beautiful apartment filled with expensive items of modern taste. She drove a modern sports car and could make minor repairs herself. Her greatest single "creative" experience was to race madly "free" down the highways, enraptured with the power and surge of her car, and with the flashing scenery.

I have written about Jean as if she were alive. She isn't. She killed herself during one compulsive ritual, racing her sports car "creatively" down the highway. This was listed as an accident, but I am not at all sure that it was.

It's unfortunate that Jean's life came to such a sorry and sudden end. She was just beginning to get in touch with herself in small ways. She was experimenting with simple habits (roles) relating to food and bath, eating at least one meal every day by herself, and taking great care to eat only when she first experienced hunger. She was establishing contact with her feelings about food by making sure she carefully tasted, smelled, and touched the food before she ate it.

She deliberately paid attention to her toilet habits. For instance, formerly she had a habit of carefully folding toilet paper a certain way before using it. She always read while on the toilet for any length of time. But she was beginning to break up this routine and to pay attention to the "feel" of herself while eliminating.

Jean gave away her cat and replaced it with a dog. She was able to treat the cat "as if it could take care of itself," but the dog needed more care and affection. She discovered she liked having the dog, a sloppy, funny-looking, mixed breed. She also discovered she really could accept children, at least certain ones. Deliberately thinking through which children around her would be easiest to be with, she chose one, the young daughter of a neighbor in the apartment, as the object of her affection. Slowly, once or twice a month, she took the child for a few hours. Jean had built up to an afternoon a week, learning to adjust herself to the child, rather than adjusting the child to fit her.

By letting the young girl determine what they would do together, Jean was beginning to learn how to relinquish her grip on herself in her personal habits concerning food and bath, and how to ease up on her harsh demands that others be a certain way. It's unfortunate that Jean came to such an abrupt and voilent end. Given patience and time, and continued practice in improving her roles, she may have found a new life.

Mark: third example of a verbal personality

Let's turn to a third example, a young man of twenty. Mark was a good student in college. While he didn't say much, he was bright, alert, and worked steadily, but not hard. Schoolwork came easily to him and he was a bit contemptuous of persons who didn't do as well as he. In fact, he was arrogant, but concealed this as best he could.

All through school he was the delight of his teachers and parents. They needed to show him what to do only once and he learned it. He not only could learn quickly but could feed back his information almost exactly as he was taught. Honors came to him in profusion.

Mark thrived when around bright persons he could imitate, and he was inclined to follow their lead. But he couldn't be innovative. He intensely disliked being alone. (This is the mark of a verbal and anomic personality. Neither wants to be alone because, when they are alone, they are *really* alone, for they are not in touch with themselves.) Mark felt comfortable only when he was able to relate to someone else who was either his superior or his inferior. No one was *equal* to Mark. They were either better or not as good.

Although Mark would rather have been superior, he was content to associate with an obviously superior person and to accept the inferior role for himself. He preferred persons much older than himself. Mark was good at mathematics, and familiar with cars and guns. A competent athlete, he excelled at contests. People around him tired of his strong, competitive sense and his compulsive need to win.

Easily bored, he became restless in the presence of others. He preferred to be in some kind of action, whatever the situation. Mark punished others with his alertness and competitive skills. He was most happy when victorious over others. When others declined to play his game, he turned to his hobbies. He "competed" by testing his skill at manipulating objects, as in target shooting with a gun. He could spend hours honing this kind of skill.

Mark's "stuck point"

Mark was not "by himself" in this activity. While target shooting, he envisioned himself beating the world champion shooter. He didn't imagine the presence of the expert, but he did "hear" words. That is, he did not create scenes—only words, a voice saying "Mark gets 299 out of 300," or something similar. At a stuck point with himself, Mark was vaguely aware that he was frequently unhappy and discontented. He carefully masturbated regularly. Although he dated now and then, he had never had intercourse. He thought that girls were *very* inferior and didn't wish to subjugate himself by pleading, which he believed was necessary to induce a girl to "give in." He believed sex relations to be a weakness, and preferred to be around men, doing manly things. Women saw Mark as somewhat sadistic and cruel.

Mark began getting in touch with himself when he got lost on a camping trip. After wandering for a day and a night, he fell and broke a leg. This brush with death created the conditions for his examining his alleged superiority over the world of objects and inferior persons. This experience shattered his verbal personality of roles. Mark was lost in more ways than one. There was no one present to show Mark what to do in a situation that demanded creative responses to solve the dilemma of being lost and hurt. Mark was a fortunate verbal to have learned so easily and so quickly.

Some verbal-anomic differences

Some of the differences between anomic and verbal personalities may be noted at this point. As shown by the descriptions of the three verbal personalities, there is a great deal of energy expended daily as verbals and anomics adjust themselves (their natural behavior) to fit roles (their personality of social behavior).

Now, the anomic tends to respond too soon to his feelings. When he eats, for instance, he reacts to the look or smell, and may lose his appetite, or reject the food on the basis of a single feeling (sensation). The anomic expends energy with these too-soon responses. His anxiety is expressed quickly as fears or guilt, and the emotional reaction is discharged. He is not acting to satisfy his need (for food in this instance). The energy is not bottled up, but discharged in incomplete responses.

In the case of the verbal personality, feelings are suppressed. If food doesn't look appetizing, he pretends it doesn't matter, or ignores how he feels about it and eats it anyway. This is significant: The verbal in his dynamic does not expend his energy in too-soon responses, but uses it to hold back his responses, to suppress his reactions. This holding-back action takes far greater energy than that expended by the anomic.

The verbal personality's energy is expended toward himself. This bottled-up aggression (of the verbal) creates anxiety which is expressed in violence toward himself, or others, or objects. Thus, the verbal discharges the energy of suppressed and delayed responses through violence. For example, Tom punished Betty and others with verbal violence. He attacked others, too, for inefficiency or lack of role organization. He punished himself severely with self-criticism.

Jean punished herself with surgery and self-hatred. And she expressed violence by means of objects, her car for instance, in which she finally died. She also punished others with her aggressive attempts to control them. Mark held himself in rigid self-control but expended his violence through objects such as guns, or games, or contests of physical and mental skill.

Violent behavior and the verbal

In nearly every case, the verbal personality is eventually caught up in some violent behavior. Tom's violence was subdued on the surface, but Jean's was pronounced: ulcers, surgery, and finally death. Mark broke a leg before he softened his aggression toward himself and others.

This pattern — suppressed feelings that accumulate to build up emotional pressures that find expression in some kind of violence — is the outstanding characteristic of the verbal personality. Such a personality suffers great pain and needs to inflict pain to find temporary relief.

The visible differences between the anomic and verbal appear in their role behavior, in how they do things, and in the group ways they have adopted for social behavior to create their personalities.

The anomic doesn't learn and adopt enough roles to organize himself, to find what group ways fit him. The verbal learns too many roles, and adopts too many ways to organize himself. Where the anomic has a scattered personality, the verbal has a rigid personality. The anomic, lacking strong roles, is unpredictable. The verbal, with rigid roles, is very predictable. Both suffer pain from being out of touch with themselves; both are alienated from their inner emotional life. But the bottled-up pain of the verbal, since it does not find release through "so many feelings" as does the anomic, creates the greater problem. The verbal has more severe problems with himself.

In an attempt to "control" his feelings, the verbal may resort to almost any means. If his pattern is one to punish himself, he will use drugs, alcohol, or rigid health regimens in an attempt to change what he is experiencing within himself and in the world about him. If necessary the verbal will attempt to break off from or change the source of sensory contact in order to control himself.

One of the more common statements made by a drug user is that the person wants to change the pain "caused" by the outside world. The verbal believes that external forces control his behavior, and he uses drugs as one external control over himself. The anomic may use drugs too, but there is not the latent violence involved in his drug use. The anomic tends to use the "softer" drugs to distort contact with the outside world. Marijuana, loud music, "busy-busy" projects, and "emotional" scenes, are more indicative of the anomic's attempts to relieve inner pain. The verbal may turn to strong drugs because his is a stronger pain. Both the anomic and verbal turn to sleep as a recourse when necessary.

Criminal activity and the verbal

Perhaps the most visible of all verbal characteristics is criminal activity. It is probable that most violent crimes are committed by verbal personalities, who are extracting vengeance on themselves or on the outer world, striking out (or back) in anger, while discharging bottled-up aggression. Boxing matches, football, baseball, wrestling matches, and auto races are not enough for many verbals. Nor can television or movies drain off enough bottled-up verbal violence. Too many verbals need more direct action.

Some verbals work through their need for aggression with the right kinds of jobs. A verbal sitting in the seat of a huge bulldozer can "change the world" for a moment; an engineer can build dams to hold water; a surgeon can "re-make" another person with a knife. Most of the world's technical progress seems to have been accomplished by verbals bent on getting things adjusted in some orderly fashion which they approve. They get things done. They relate better to a world of objects and things, where emotions don't clutter up the picture.

The anomic experiences pain, is hurt, and gets hostile and angry more easily, but generally ends up hurting himself more than others. The verbal must master not only himself but others, too. The verbal's organization of himself generally includes the organization of everyone around him. Frequently, others suffer the verbal's pain.

Neither the verbal nor the anomic is a self-regulating person. Both look to outside events, or external situations, to determine what happens to them. The anomic sees unknown forces quite beyond his control acting on him, and shaping his destiny. The verbal internalizes group ways (roles) and uses these as his "external" control of himself. The results are the same. Each type of person becomes alienated from himself, out of touch with the dynamic flow of feelings that grows into full emotional responses — the creative act that integrates, or brings together, his natural and social behavior.

General traits of verbals

Let's review some of the more general traits of the verbal personality. He tends to be *over-integrated* with social behavior, and to suppress his natural behavior. He has too much personality, too many roles. The verbal tends not to respond to his feelings, but to *suppress feelings* before they grow into an emotional response. He tends to be role-bound, rather than roleless, and past rather than present oriented. He believes customs and traditions are to be trusted, and feelings and emotions are to be ignored as untrustworthy.

The verbal *relates better to objects or things* than to persons. He is efficient, but also tends to punish himself or others. He believes he should adjust himself to fit his personality and that others should adjust themselves to fit his roles. He adjusts well to situations where there is a fixed or preordained pattern for persons or things. The verbal is too *self-controlled*, too rigid, too compulsive in behavior. He expresses anxiety with violence toward himself, others, or objects. The verbal likes violence.

The verbal lacks imagination; he seldom daydreams or invents "unreal" situations with his inner thoughts. He relies on "facts." He wants to be objective, to remove himself from reality, and above all, to be impersonal, formal, and "fair." He believes the natural, impersonal external world rewards those who manipulate themselves and others to fit this objective process. *Pragmatic, realistic, objective, scientific,* and *reality* are terms favored by the verbal personality.

Are you an anomic or a verbal?

Many persons have difficulty in deciding whether they tend to be over- or under-integrated, with verbal or anomic personalities. A common statement is, "I feel that I have both of these tendencies, that sometimes I'm fairly anomic and at other times more verbal."

As may be seen, most persons are born with tendencies to be either over- or under-integrated with their social behavior. Very few persons learn how to integrate their natural and social behavior without learning what to do and how to do it. Everyone is a mixture of over- and under-integration, but one or the other will emerge as dominant in behavior. Everyone is struggling with his own tendencies, his own unique mixture of natural and social behavior. Infants and young children seem more anomic than verbal because of their lack of socialization with roles. But very soon, the "personality" appears in behavior. A young person may think through which kind of personality he is creating for himself as easily as an older person.

If you respond too soon to your feelings, if you tend to be disorganized with yourself, if you like persons rather than things, if you have a poor "object" memory for dates, time, and distance, you are anomic. You prefer informal relationships.

If you are well-organized, handy with objects, facts, and figures, have a good social personality, feel uncomfortable when other persons cry or show "feelings," and have a good "object" memory, you are a verbal. You prefer formal relationships.

I sometimes envision this world as a huge stage with anomic and verbal actors playing out their personality of roles in a continuing comedy (tragedy?) of errors: The verbals launch a space ship that blows up because an anomic failed to tighten a screw. I see these incredibly different personalities in a continual contest, struggling with one another, not really knowing why their common efforts seem to fail so miserably. I see the verbal chastising the anomic everywhere for "screwing up the works." I see the anomic attempting to curb the verbal, and to restrain his excesses.

In the next chapter, I examine how the anomic or verbal goes about getting in touch with himself.

4

Getting in Touch
With Yourself

The first step in getting in touch with yourself is to determine whether you have lost contact with your inner world of feelings and emotions or your outer world of persons, things, or events. Marjorie, a young woman of twenty-four, is an example of a person who had lost touch with her outer world of persons and events, her external world. She had spent most of her life in a church school and convent. She left the convent and tried to create a new life for herself.

Marjorie had dedicated herself to a life within the church. This role did not fit her and she suffered daily pain. She did not feel she was a good enough person to become a nun and much of her personal behavior caused her to be plagued with feelings of fear and guilt.

After abandoning her only major role in life, that of a nun, Marjorie suffered an even greater pain. She was like a boat that lost not only its rudder but its anchor too, and drifts free; she was buffeted by waves of emotion beyond her control. She lived in fear, afraid to respond with confidence to anyone or anything because she couldn't trust herself to handle the decisions she wanted to make.

Marjorie found refuge in sleep. She could sleep ten, twelve, or more hours a day. She used sleep as a drug to escape from pain. The only relationship she had was with a girl friend with whom she shared an apartment. Marjorie clung to this friend, her anchor in her personal storm. Marjorie finally (through her friend's efforts) found a young man who interested her very much, and with whom she had her first sexual encounter.

Marjorie was delighted with her experience. She had never satisfied herself in such a fulfilling way. Furthermore, it seemed an answer to another problem that bothered her very much. She had masturbated regularly for four or five years and was increasingly concerned about the variety of objects and methods she used in her solitary sexual activity. Her new boy friend saw her only twice and then faded out and didn't come back. Marjorie felt she was at fault, somehow. The young man didn't say so, but she sensed that he thought she was a "cold fish." This frightened and puzzled her since she was really thrilled by her sexual experience and felt no need for solitary sex for several days after her first encounter.

How did Marjorie take the first step toward getting in touch with herself — to understand where she had lost contact with her outer world, her external life?

Marjorie was born with tendencies which made it difficult for her to integrate her outer world of experience with her inner world of feelings and emotions, that is, to combine her natural and social behavior. She had never understood well how to do things for herself, to adopt roles, and to practice these group ways of doing things until she molded them to fit herself.

Marjorie tended to adopt inadequate ways of doing things that didn't fit her needs. She tended to be an under-integrated person, one who didn't learn how to cope with the external world. Saying it another way, Marjorie was born with tendencies to relate more to her inner world of feelings and emotions than to her outer world of external events.

Marjorie was vaguely aware that her convent life didn't fit her. She realized that she did not relate well to objects or things, to abstract ideas and structures, or the *impersonal* ways of life that dominated her day-to-day routine. Marjorie understood that she related best to people in a *personal,* informal way.

Her life in the convent required her to relate to impersonal relationships, rituals, robes, and abstract ideas. Marjorie couldn't relate to a God she couldn't see, or touch, or talk with face-to-face. She blamed herself and tried to cram her inner responses into a role of "being a nun" in her outer world. She couldn't absorb the role of being a nun because of her inner feelings and emotional reactions.

Finally Marjorie awakened to the incongruity of her unhappy situation. She realized that something was very wrong and began to make changes. She left the convent but blamed herself for being a failure. Nevertheless, she had taken the first step in the right direction. She had to look for a way of life in which she could relate directly to persons and not to some formal role relationship in the form of a job or duty.

The first step: A new career

After some searching, Marjorie decided in favor of a future which, she felt, would fulfill her needs. She found a "fit" for herself by becoming a student working toward a teaching career. Teaching is a job which has many formal roles, but it also allowed Marjorie to relate directly, face-to-face, with persons rather than objects or things. Marjorie could be very creative and stay in touch with herself in her new role as a teacher.

This for Marjorie was the first big step: to anchor herself in her outer world of experience with a role that fitted her natural need to relate to persons rather than objects or abstract ideas. Although this was just the first step, it was crucial. Marjorie needed to discover ways of getting in touch with herself whereby she could sort out her various feelings about things that happened to her in her outside world. She had always had many feelings that she couldn't understand and didn't know what to do about.

To get in touch and stay in touch, Marjorie had to be able to sort out how she felt about her experiences. Her new role as a student working toward a teaching career anchored her and gave her time to begin some sensory exercises that helped her link her inner and outer world. This was a vital move in her finding herself, as we shall see.

A combination of exercises helps unify inner and outer experiences

Marjorie tried a variety of sensory awareness experiments before she found the right combination that helped her integrate herself, or unify her inner and outer experiences. I will describe a range of these sensory awareness experiments in later paragraphs but for now let's examine the ones that worked for Marjorie. When you see how they work, you'll understand better why they work. These are simple breathing, relaxing, and talking exercises which she used to establish good, clear contact with the outer world. Whenever she felt she was losing contact, or getting out of touch with the outer world, she merely increased the time she spent with her sensory exercises.

Marjorie found that her anxiety was always linked with her holding her breath and tensing her body muscles in a painful clinch. She made this discovery after several weeks of experimenting. Then she practiced different ways of sensory contacts before she found her right combination. Marjorie combined breathing exercises with relaxing exercises. She was accustomed to taking a shower but she changed this habit (role) to taking a full bath. Each evening she filled her tub with very warm water and submerged herself to soak. She became aware of how the water felt over her entire body. She swirled the water in and around her limbs, floating her hands, sometimes her legs.

Then she deliberately relaxed each part of her body that seemed tense, and tried to notice those parts she had never really sensed before. She thought about how her back felt for the first time, and then worked to relax her back muscles.

She practiced "out-loud" breathing. She inhaled deep lungfuls of air and exhaled them vigorously, noticing and feeling the rush of air in and out her body. She even shouted a bit when she felt the air surge in and out. She would stick her head under water and see how long she could hold her breath. She inhaled and exhaled hard enough sometimes to make her dizzy.

Her most important discovery came after she had learned how to breath and relax her body. *She learned to sort out her feelings and find words to fit her feelings and verbally express them.* This was an act of creative integration that unified her inner and outer world. After a few minutes in the tub, Marjorie would think through some recent experience of high emotional conflict. She would recreate in her mind the event surrounding this emotional conflict. As her feelings rose, she slowly sorted them out one at a time, and found words to fit the sensations. As the words came to her mind, she said them out loud — that is, she talked to herself.

Finding words for feelings is difficult

She talked to herself out loud until she found the words that fit her feelings. Sometimes this was hard to do, but she persisted until she was aware that she had found the right words to fit the feeling. For instance, Marjorie had strong unfinished emotional conflicts over her brief affair and her solitary sexuality. Lying in her tub, relaxed, breathing deeply, she let these two unfinished emotional conflicts struggle to the surface of her awareness.

She realized masturbation bothered her more than her brief affair; at least, this conflict popped into her mind quicker than her sexual activity with the young man. She began working through her feelings about her solitary sex and finding words to express them.

She berated herself out loud, made cruel fun of herself for using objects (a teddy bear, a small vibrator) to gratify her need. She kept talking this through, finding torrents of words to fit the surge of feelings that flooded her mind. One evening, she found she had difficulty finding the right words. The reason was that new feelings had begun to surface, and she had to invent new descriptions to fit them. Now she talked with those new feelings – with her inner experience with herself. She was making progress.

Marjorie found herself talking out loud about love, and her need to love, and about someone to love her in return. This brought a sudden insight: she realized that her solitary sex was pleasurable but totally inadequate to meet her real needs. She wanted to love someone and be loved in return. Although her sexual affair with the young man was even more pleasing than masturbation, it too was inadequate compared with what she really wanted.

She learned that *very few persons* really attracted her sexually, and just as important, that she shouldn't attempt to relate emotionally to persons when this attraction didn't exist. This was her most self-defeating trait – trying to relate emotionally to someone when she felt no physical attraction for him. (This is true for both women and men, but with a different sexual component for the male.)

Marjorie failed in her relationships with persons because she wanted to create emotional relationships that *she couldn't feel herself.* The young man sensed this apparently; he perhaps wanted love, too. But their sexual encounter was a counterfeit relationship for both.

Trusting in feelings

Marjorie learned to trust her own feelings about a person and not to get involved unless there was a definite attraction for her, whether the person be a man or a woman. This was especially important if a man were someone with whom she might enter a full sexual relationship. If Marjorie started a relationship in which she didn't feel this attraction, she was caught in her own personality trap.

For instance, if Marjorie were to marry, she had better marry a man who was strongly attractive to her physically as well as mentally. The sexual component of love would be necessary for love to exist between her and a man. That is, strong sexual feelings would be needed to give rise to the full emotion of love. Sexual feelings are only a part of this emotion, which includes feelings of security, belonging, closeness, and so on. But the sexual feelings are imperative. You can have sex without love, but not love without sex, as the saying goes.

Strong attraction is necessary

Marjorie had to be careful about getting into relationships where there was not strong physical attraction on her part for the other person. Although a man had good role attributes — handsome, good provider, stable, interesting — Marjorie's day-to-day need was to relate to the person emotionally. If she couldn't, she got out of touch with herself, and alienated from her outer world. And she needlessly blamed herself when this occurred.

Marjorie could not relate to other persons in roles, the formal group ways of doing things impersonally. She needed to touch and pat and feel other persons, to feel that they were *real* and that she was *real,* not counterfeit. She reassured herself by doing this.

If she was not attracted to a person, she would try to touch too much, or she would demand too much attention, attempts to make sure that she was there and that she was real. This was a trap Marjorie had to avoid setting for herself. If she was not strongly attracted to a person, she would smother their relationship with unreasonable demands. This was true in friendships with women, men, children, animals, and things. Marjorie shouldn't have worn or used a thing that she didn't strongly care for.

Having learned her lessons well, Marjorie dropped several relationships when she discovered she was not strongly attracted to the people. She didn't make friends easily, but she had two very close girl friends and was quite interested in another male. When she got out of touch with herself, it was "back to the tub" for Marjorie. She had learned *how and what to do* to link her inner and outer worlds – to get in touch with herself.

Marjorie was fortunate to find a couple of easy sensory exercises so quickly (within three weeks) that aided her so much so soon. Most persons have to work through much more and experiment more with themselves. Breaking out of the personality trap isn't always that easy.

A second example: Paul

A man in his early thirties, let's call him Paul, is a rather good example of a person who got in touch with himself. Paul was a successful school psychologist. He did not relate well to the outer world of persons and things outside his job. His job fitted him because he related warmly in face-to-face encounters with persons in his office. That is, Paul only related to persons when he was acting in his role of psychologist. He did not make good contact with the outer world outside of this role.

This situation irritated and alienated Paul's wife, friends, children, and coworkers. When Paul's wife demanded that he quit "psyching her out" and relate to her as a real person who happened to be his wife, Paul fell apart. He knew he was in the wrong. He blamed himself but seemed compulsively unable to "stop himself" from dealing this way with everyone as time went on.

Getting in touch for Paul took considerable and continued effort. It involved a number of steps which affected his appearance, behavior, and habits. First, he threw away more than a hundred books, and the stacks of journals which he'd never read and was just hoarding, keeping them on the shelf as visible props for his psychologist role. He tossed out a dozen pipes, which he really didn't like to smoke.

Continuing the metamorphosis, he shaved off his mustache and long sideburns. He didn't like either of them, he discovered, after he began getting in closer touch with himself. They were more props for his psychologist role. He bought clothes that he liked, and discarded his "psychologist" flashy, mod clothes. All this activity just cleared the decks for the real work with himself. Like an actor completing a stage role, he stripped off his makeup and costume and tried to see himself as he really was.

Even at this point, Paul was not aware of the priority of his needs, a common problem for someone out of touch with the outer world. Paul didn't know what he wanted to do from day to day, outside of his school psychology job. He didn't even know what he needed to do; therefore he would let the decisions be made by his wife or whoever else was concerned.

I should point out that a person becomes aware of his needs only after he has experienced an emotional response. Emotions flow from feelings that arise from a variety of sensations that might be happening in a person. A person doesn't have an emotional response to hunger for food, for instance, until he feels the sensations rising from this need.

Experiments for getting in touch

Paul's getting-in-touch experiments dealt with his eating habits and his contacts with objects — all the inanimate things that he used or was in contact with in some way in his outer world. He began eating lunch by himself, so that he wouldn't feel embarrassed by his "getting in touch with food" experiment. He waited to eat only after he experienced hunger. Then he bought only the food that looked *very* good to him. Paul tended to *respond too soon* to the slightest negative feeling so was careful to eat only the food that looked good to him. Also, he began eating slowly. He smelled the food — brought it to his nostrils for a whiff before each bite. Sometimes he touched the food, even tore it up before eating, always making sure he had good clear sensory contact with the food before he put it in his mouth. He tasted each bite, chewed slowly, savored the flavor, and felt the food go down when he swallowed it.

This is the specific dynamic of what Paul did to integrate his inner experience with the outer world and get in touch with himself: He made sure he was acting *with an inner need.* In the case just cited, his inner need was hunger for food. Then Paul made certain that the object of his need in the outer world, food, *fitted his need:* that the food looked, smelled, felt, and tasted good, and that he fully experienced these sensations (feelings) so that he could have the emotional response of gratification of his hunger.

A felt experience

This acting with experience and feeling, linking inner need with the outer world, allowed the creative, unifying, integrating process. All of the sensory contacts with food gave rise to Paul's feelings, the sensations of touch, smell, and taste; and as these feelings converged, they formed an emotional response which organized Paul to have a *felt experience.*

This, then, was an integrated act, moving from stimulus to feelings to an emotional response in one unified pattern that linked (integrated) Paul's inner and outer worlds. It was a creative act for Paul (or anyone), an act which integrated Paul's behavior and got him in touch with himself. He learned how to do this when dealing with his food, and this experience gave him confidence to experiment with less obvious situations.

Paul had a terrible memory. He tended to live in the future, and did not make good contact with experiences in the present. Consequently, experiences that flowed from the present to become the past were difficult to recall.

Creative acts integrated his past experiences with his present behavior. When this occurred, he "remembered better." Paul did not experience much happening in him in the present; this situation was alienating, and was responsible for much of his pain.

Paul deliberately began playing with the objects in his outer world with which he came into contact during the day. He picked up his telephone receiver, gripped it as hard as he could, and banged it gently against his desk top to hear its hardness. He pretended it was a club, then he unscrewed the ear and mouth pieces, and looked at the insides. He imagined the telephone not black but white with purple polka dots.

He took a pencil in his hand and tried to think of how many uses other than writing the pencil had, or how many other persons were using a pencil at that moment all over the world. All of the objects and things that Paul was in daily contact with — used, touched, or was close to — got this kind of fantasy-in-the-present treatment.

But perhaps the most significant dynamic for Paul was his talking out loud about *how he was experiencing* the various objects in his outer world. He also did this with his food experiences. He expressed his thoughts verbally, talked out loud to himself, and described how and what he was feeling at the moment, whatever he was doing.

Becoming anchored in the present

Paul discovered that by talking out loud *with his experience* (how he felt about whatever he was doing in his contacts with objects) the experience was creatively integrated. By talking with his current experience, Paul was *anchored in the present.* This allowed his feelings to grow into an emotional response that integrated his past experience with his present behavior, and his inner and outer worlds.

For example, while toying with his telephone one day, talking out loud with his rising feelings, Paul discovered he did not like telephones, had never liked them, and did not talk well over them. Consequently, he had avoided many situations that required talking on the phone, often to his disadvantage. (Paul's wife had stopped trying to talk over a phone with him years before.)

The sudden discovery that he disliked telephones grew out of hundreds of unfinished emotional responses he had accumulated. And nearly every day new ones joined the other debris. Then came this insight, nurtured by the idea of talking out loud to himself about his feelings. This insight came after many weeks of deliberate experimenting. Almost by itself it gave Paul a massive boost of self-confidence and encouraged him to experiment more with himself.

Paul found out what to do to integrate himself, to get in touch with himself. His friends thought he was a little crazy, talking to his food and talking to himself or things every once in a while. But he discovered and "finished" several unfinished emotional areas. For one, he found that if he "had it out" with a telephone before he used it, that is, before he dialed, he could "be himself" when he dealt with the person he was calling. He berated the phone if he felt like it: "I don't like you, telephone, because I would rather talk with the person face-to-face, and telephones don't permit that." Out loud. Silent scolding, Paul found, didn't link his inner feelings with how he was experiencing the telephone, that object in his outer world. The sound of his own voice made the experience feel real for him.

His verbal expression was a creative act that linked his inner and outer experiences. When he found words that fitted how he felt inside about something outside, his worlds became integrated. In some instances, Paul found he could accomplish this by silently expressing his feelings about an outer event, but he preferred the "verbal" path whenever possible. While he shaved, he talked out loud about how he felt while shaving and looking in the mirror. He linked what he was doing at the moment with his inner feelings by expressing himself out loud.

Similarities in Marjorie and Paul

Let us pause for a moment to consider what's revealed in the examples of Marjorie and Paul, two apparently different kinds of persons with different problems. There are basic similarities in how they got to be the way they were, and what they did to get in touch with themselves.

First, they were born with tendencies that made it difficult for them to link their outer world with their inner experiences. This meant they did not integrate their learned outward behavior (their social behavior) with their inner natural behavior. They did not make clear, firm contact with the outer world.

They did not relate well to objects, or things. Both had a few possessions they felt strongly about — a pair of shoes, a favorite piece of furniture, or something of the sort. But mostly, they felt real only when they could relate directly, informally, and personally to other persons who related in the same way with them.

It is very difficult for people who are out of contact with the outer world to adopt roles, and to practice those ways of doing things that fit them. Consequently, they develop inadequate personalities (weak or inadequate roles of social behavior, the anomic personality described earlier). It is essential that, when they adopt roles, they adopt ones in which they can feel strong personal attraction for the person or persons in the relationship. If they are involved in a relationship and are not supported by this unifying emotional contact, they become alienated and painfully out of touch with themselves.

Formal role behavior is treacherous for someone who is out of touch with his external world. He tends to be roleless in his natural behavior.

Limiting the number of roles

One of the most important hazards that Paul and Marjorie had to avoid was taking on too many roles. Neither one could handle a lot of impersonal role relationships. This meant they should not have too many friends because they couldn't relate strongly to more than a few persons at any given time in life. One lover, one spouse, a couple of children, one or two close friends, a few more casual friends, were generally all that could be coped with. They could have lots of love but this love needed to thrive in a small, closely-knit outer world.

They needed clear-cut, well-defined boundaries in their outer world of persons and things in order to stay in touch with themselves. Marjorie couldn't handle being in love with more than one boy at a time. Two boy friends at the same time would have devastated her because of her own real feelings of attraction to both.

When at home, Paul felt most content when he ate dinner with his wife after the children had been fed. He felt better when he took his children somewhere one at a time, not all three on the same outing. He got out of touch with how he felt when he had more than one person at a time to relate to. His person-to-person psychologist's job fitted this tendency neatly, for he was creative and competent when he was working with one person at a time. Marjorie would be successful in a teacher's role if she did not try to relate to a whole classroom of children, but rather to pupils, one at a time.

Persons who have lost touch with their outer world, like Marjorie and Paul had, tend to respond too soon, with their feelings rather than with emotions. Feelings are the beginning of emotions; they precede an emotional response. Emotions grow out of feelings. For example, Marjorie tended to respond too soon to her food, which may have had a bland appearance, but tasted and smelled good to her when she ate it. Instead of waiting until she smelled and tasted the food, she reacted to her feelings toward its bland appearance. Several feelings must converge to produce an emotional reaction. By responding to the food's blandness, Marjorie had an incomplete experience with her food.

Getting in touch with her outer world consisted of making good, clear contacts with persons, objects, and activities. Marjorie could have practiced this while, say, driving a car. She could have talked with her experiences out loud to herself as they occurred in the present moment. For example, she might have said: "I am now getting in the car. The car smells smoky and funny. I must get it washed. I am starting the engine and backing out the driveway. I am sitting on the buckle of my seat belt and it hurts. I am shifting the automatic into drive. Now I am driving east, toward town." Though it may seem ridiculous, this running, spoken commentary anchors the person in his outer world, and gives him a chance to sort out the rising feelings that build into emotional responses. For instance, as Marjorie drove to school, she might have said: "I am approaching that bad intersection where I was nearly hit yesterday. I was sure frightened then. I'm scared now. I'm as frightened as I was yesterday. I will slow down and be very cautious as I go through this intersection."

Marjorie was talking with the various feelings she was experiencing as they gave rise to an emotion of fear. She got in touch with herself as she got the *feel* of how her various feelings grew inside her as a result of her experiences in the outer world.

The talking out loud, the finding of words to fit this rise of feelings that were growing into an emotional reaction, linked Marjorie's inner and outer world for her. *This is the single most important getting-in-touch exercise.* Once Marjorie learned to do this by herself, she could find ways to speak with people. Again, it was a matter of finding the right words to fit her feelings and the emotions that finally occurred.

Persons out of touch with their *inner world* have a different dynamic to deal with in getting in touch with themselves. Where Marjorie and Paul had too many "feelings," a person who has lost touch with his inner world has too few.

A description of Bill, a man out of touch with his inner world

Bill was a personnel officer with a large industrial firm. He was twenty-eight and married, with three children. He liked his job. He had a secretary, a small but comfortable office, and four persons working under him in his section. Bill liked the formal, well-organized daily routine and enjoyed making decisions about hiring and firing and putting the "right person" in the right job. He liked the paperwork and the conferences and the interviewing activity, especially when looking over the hundreds of applications filled out by job seekers.

Bill had a verbal personality. He was very much out of touch with his inner world of feelings and emotions. He worried about this for several reasons, but mostly because he didn't understand why he failed to experience things the way his wife, friends, and coworkers seemed to. His wife Charlene, for instance, would occasionally burst into tears over some matter or other. Bill would not have the slightest idea why she was upset. He was sympathetic and concerned, but he never really understood, even after she explained her reason for being disturbed.

All in all, Bill thought his life was great. Now and then other persons got very angry with him and "told him off," which caused him fleeting but real concern. To get in touch with himself, to discover his inner world of feelings and emotions, involved some very hard work and persistence.

The problem of suppressed feelings

Bill had to learn how to get the feel of his body, and how he felt inside about the things that were happening to him. Like Marjorie and Paul, he did not experience emotional reactions, but for a different reason. Whereas anomics Marjorie and Paul responded too soon to their feelings, before the feelings built into an emotional response, verbal Bill suppressed his feelings. He didn't let them grow to become an emotional reaction.

So Bill's getting-in-touch experiments involved making contact with his inner experiences. There were several areas that Bill experimented with in his practice with himself before he discovered the richness of his inner life of feelings and emotions.

The exercises that worked for Bill included sensory work in eating, eliminating, touching, and sexual behavior. I will describe what he accomplished in each area, emphasizing that he got results only after much work and a somewhat uneven success for several months. But he gained nearly immediately after he started his exercises, for change in any one area helps bring about change in the others.

Bill learned to *attend* to his food. Even when busy or in a rush, he took time to make good contact with what he ate. Like Marjorie and Paul, he learned to talk out loud as feelings arose; in his case, to talk about his feelings about his inner world. He found words to fit his feelings about food, instead of ignoring them as he once did.

He talked to his food: "I guess I don't like mustard dripping off my plate. I do like hot dogs. I like this hot dog. It smells good and tastes good, if I don't eat it too fast. Hot dogs cooking on a grill always remind me of a skinny penis."

A flow of thoughts like these came hard for Bill. He had to "let go" and find words to fit the vague and fleeting sensations or feelings that arose from his inner experience. He felt absurd at first and had difficulty continuing the eating experiments until they began to have an effect. He touched his food, and talked to it; he *had his experience with it* before he gulped it down, however he felt. And he described it out loud.

Bill changed his toilet habits. He was used to ignoring what he was doing while eliminating. So he practiced being aware of the feel of his urine and noticed its feel, color, and his ability to speed up or slow down its flow. He learned to play with the stream, and remembered how he had done this as a child.

Bill concentrated on his bowel movements, deliberately tried to feel his bowels inside him. He noticed how it felt as his muscles contracted to pass the matter through his system. He felt the matter pass through his anal opening. He took time to learn to get the feel of himself this way, to talk out loud about it and find words to fit his feelings.

Touch exercises are significant

Perhaps the most significant exercises for Bill dealt with his touching other persons, and with his sexual behavior. He had to make a start in his inner sexual life before he could make progress in his touching exercises.

Bill had "good control" of himself when he and Charlene

had sex. He promptly had an erection and could sustain it for an hour (or more) before he permitted himself to have an orgasm. Charlene had great difficulty adjusting herself at first because she would experience a full orgasm within a few minutes, and would have preferred to stop and rest. But Bill had a sex role for himself of the virile man "taking good care of his wife." This role was fulfilled by making sure he lasted, and lasted, and lasted, until Charlene pleaded with him to finish—that she had "had enough."

Bill was disappointed, if not surprised, that Charlene began avoiding sex with him. She said that she was too tired, or not in the mood, or too busy. Actually, she cared little about her husband's sexual prowess and stamina. Furthermore, her idea of sex wasn't related to watching a clock. What she wanted was that her husband touch and feel her with his hand. And, she wanted to respond in the same way, not only in bed but elsewhere during the day.

She liked to be fondled, hugged, and fussed over in the kitchen, on the sofa, anywhere. However, it wasn't in Bill's makeup to pat, pinch, stroke, hug, and nibble his mate's ear. Nor did he want these endearing things done to him. At least, he didn't think they mattered much.

Charlene loved to "groom" Bill, and wanted to be groomed in return. She like to examine his face or back, squeeze pimples, or just massage him gently.

Results of Bill's work

One night, rather suddenly, Bill threw off his sex role of the masterful, virile male. He began his sexual and touching experiments, a complete turnabout. He was sitting on the edge of the bed when Charlene gently touched and held his penis in her hand. He realized it was the first time he had really *felt* the touch of her hand—really felt the smoothness, and warmth and "niceness" of his wife's touch. This was a break-through. He discovered he liked to be touched by her. He was able to *feel* her touch, whereas he had never noticed it before.

To his delight, and emotional sense of well-being, Bill also found that he liked to touch others, and to be touched by them. He found there was feeling in the simple act of shaking hands. At the office, he would briefly touch his secretary, or pat an employee on the arm. When paying a check, he'd touch the cashier's hand. It gave him pleasure to have someone help him put on his coat. He was even aware of the touch of the barber who trimmed his hair. He found every opportunity to make touch contacts.

His relations at home improved considerably. No longer did Charlene find excuses for avoiding sex. The touch experiments led to satisfying her need for love and care. We might say she benefited as much as her husband.

Mary Lou: A verbal personality

Mary Lou was another example of a person out of touch with her inner world of feelings and emotions, a verbal personality. She was around forty, wealthy, had had two marriages and had been drinking heavily for many years. She alternated between drugs and alcohol, and preferred whisky. (People who are out of touch with their inner world can suffer much pain and may make great efforts to block sensory contact with their inner life.)

For most of her life Mary Lou had pretended she didn't have feelings. She suppressed her feelings about her daily experiences. Feelings hurt so she tried to kill them or to block her awareness of them. She used drugs and liquor to break off contact with her inner world. This seems to be a common, popular way of getting out of touch with oneself.

Mary Lou had a single exercise that got her started on the way to getting in touch with herself; she recaptured unpleasant experiences in her imagination and worked through her feelings in detail. This was very hard work for her.

The exercise is easy to describe: Mary Lou sat or lay down, and recalled her most recent painful experience. She recaptured in detail everything she could, as if it were happening at the moment.

Then, slowly, she found words to fit each sensation, vague or clear, that formed during her fantasy of the past experience. Crucial to the success of this imagining process was learning to let the *images of the experience* flow before choosing words to fit the feelings.

This meant that Mary Lou had to learn to first suppress her thinking in terms of words; that is, clear her mind of conscious words to let the images rise. Her feelings arose in response to the *images* (mental pictures of events or things) before she chose new words to fit the feelings invoked by those images. For example, instead of a fantasy wherein she tried to recall words that were said, she suppressed the words and fantasied the image of the person speaking, the color of his hair, the shape of his face. She concentrated on the objects, forms, and imagery of her inner impressions and thoughts, let the mental pictures occur, and *then* found words to describe the feelings she had about the mental images. Whenever Mary Lou could imagine or mentally picture an unpleasant experience as if it were occurring at that moment, then become aware of her feeling about those pictures, then talk out loud with that feeling, and describe the feeling, she got in touch with herself.

This became a dramatic experience for Mary Lou. She found she couldn't do it with another person, that is, she couldn't "talk it out" with a close friend. She would recapture her unpleasant experiences with words that didn't fit her true feelings if she tried to work through her problems with a friend or acquaintance. Suffice it to say that Mary Lou, working alone, did indeed get in touch with herself. It was a long step toward her finding purpose in life and overcoming her reliance on drugs and alcohol.

Both sexes may be out of touch

The above examples of Bill and Mary Lou, and the earlier ones of Marjorie and Paul, describe persons of both sexes who were out of touch with their outer world or with their inner world.

There seem to be significant similarities between males and females that should be noted before moving on. Members of either sex may have problems in their inner or outer worlds of experience. Males tend to get out of touch with their inner world of feelings and emotions as often as do females. And females tend to get out of touch with their outer world as often as do males. Put in another way, males and females in equal numbers are out of touch with their inner life. And as many females as males are out of touch with their outer life. These are biological and psychogenic tendencies that are determined by genes.

Exercises in sensory awareness

Now I shall describe a series of exercises, or experiments, in sensory awareness and contact for the male and female who have lost touch with their inner or outer worlds. One important point of this chapter, to be drawn from the specific examples describing different persons, is that each person will have his own unique combination of exercises, and he may have to try out different ones to find those that fit him. You will know you are on the right track when one of these exercises helps you to see things (your mental imagery) or feel things more clearly than before.

Another important point is not to force things to happen. Let them occur on their own accord and in their own time. Feelings and emotions build up by their own strength. You do not have to manufacture them. They happen on their own if you stand aside and let them go. You can't peer into yourself and say, "I'm going to have some feelings now." It doesn't work that way. You will block the rise of feelings if you analyze, introspect, and otherwise look inside yourself to find out what's going on.

The correct way is to play a waiting game. Wait for sensations to appear, *notice* what's going on in your inner or outer worlds without directing it. For example, feelings from your inner world arise from a need, such as hunger for food, which you begin to notice when you get sensations or feelings of hunger. You can't force yourself to be hungry; the hunger occurs all by itself. You can't force yourself to be in love; the love occurs all by itself. They arise from a variety of feelings inside you, which come from inner needs.

Events from the outer world also give rise to feelings that may or may not be connected directly to the event. You may see a person crying and feel sad in sympathy before you realize that the person may be crying out of happiness.

The right combination of exercises is most important

Whether you are more out of touch with your inner or your outer world is not as important as experimenting to find the right combination of sensory awareness exercises that fit your particular needs. In general, a person out of touch with his outer world (an anomic) needs to concentrate on how he makes clear contact with objects, persons, or events, in his day-to-day life. A person out of touch with his inner world (a verbal) needs to discover *how he feels inside* about the contacts he is making with objects, persons, and events in his outer world. The former works on *establishing contact with the outer world; the latter works on discovering how he feels* about his contacts with the outer world.

People may invent their own exercises, but the exercises that follow are suggested. They will start either kind of person on the road to getting in touch with himself:

Breathing. Sit, stand, or lie down and practice taking in deep lungsful of air. Concentrate on inhaling as much air as you possibly can, and then letting out as much as you possibly can. Try to collapse your lungs on exhale, expelling every last breath. Try this when you are nervous, tense, or excited. (Do it when you have a few, quiet minutes to yourself, too!)

Relaxing. Along with the breathing exercise, learn to get the feel of relaxing the specific muscles that are tense. You have to begin by noticing those tense muscles. Then talk out loud with yourself. Talk to the specific muscle. Concentrate on it, envision it in your mind and direct it to relax.

Bathing. Preferably, this exercise should be done along with the breathing and relaxing exercises. Most persons report more success when they are done in combination. But don't go to sleep (this happens to some, but these are *awareness* exercises, not attempts to blackout with sleep). Don't read or eat or do anything that takes your attention away from the exercises. Run a full tub of water, warm as possible without being too hot for you. Submerge yourself; you are changing the environment in contact with your skin from air to water. Then go through the breathing and relaxing exercises.

Mental envisioning. This exercise may also be tried with the combination above, but it is important to do it whenever possible. Clear your mind of all thoughts, all inner silent talking and forming of words. Let mental images appear. This is difficult for many. Often people wash their minds free of thoughts just before going to sleep. This is the first step in the mental envisioning exercise, but rather than preparation for sleep, the purpose is to achieve a dream-awake state. This is tricky, and may require lots of practice. But it's one of the more creative exercises for getting in touch with yourself.

Eating. Use all your senses to make good, clear contact with the food you eat. Smell, taste, touch, hear and look at your food as you eat it. Tear it up (if you find it displeasing) before you eat it. Be sure you "destroy" the food before swallowing it, either with your knife and fork or your hands before you put it in your mouth, or with your teeth before you swallow it. Do not try to talk with someone, or read, or daydream when you are eating. Attend *only* to your experiences with the food. You cannot get in touch with yourself if you diminish your awareness of this very fundamental creative act. Eat by yourself as much as possible until you can make good contact with food. Eat only what you like, and only when you're hungry.

Eliminating. As with eating, don't read, eat, or daydream about other things when you are eliminating. Let flow the rich, mental imagery of how your body feels during elimination. Get the sense, the feel, of the urine or fecal matter passing through your system and out the body openings. Also don't try to "go to the toilet" until you feel a need to do so, and then go as often as the need appears. The sensory joy of eliminating, ignored by many persons, produces fertile inner imagery.

Touching. Make firm, clear touch contacts with the objects and persons you are around daily. With objects, get the feel of hardness or softness, and the rough or smooth texture of their surfaces. Decide what feels best to you — cotton or wool, wood or metal. Do you prefer grainy or smooth surfaces? Feel your clothes when you put them on, and don't deny their contact the rest of the day. Notice your clothes binding your body, touching you in different places from time to time. Do you wear things that you don't like the feel of? Do you use a telephone and not notice its hardness?

Find sociable ways to touch persons you are with for long periods of time. Don't be near someone, talking or working or listening, without finding a way to make touch contact. This may make you feel uneasy at first, but find a way to do it that fits each situation. Inability to simply touch one another keeps people out of contact perhaps more than any other single thing.

Sexual contact. Don't have a continuing sexual relationship with someone unless the person is strongly attractive to you — to the full range of your senses. The person should smell good, look good, taste good, and feel good to your touch. If you are not determined and aggressive about this, you will have incomplete and unfelt sexual experiences. Sexual activity may be the most emotionally crippling action you can be involved in, but it may also be your most creative sensory experience. Ignore any one of your senses, and the sexual experience is distorted.

You can get out of touch with yourself quicker in your sexual contacts than in any other sensory experience. If you do not act on your sexual needs, these unresolved needs will *block* the emergence of *all* your other needs. Sexual needs will not subside or get out of the way so that you can make good contact with other emerging needs. The smell, the look, the feel, the taste—the chemistry of male and female—are very different and are the bases of attraction. Their differences complement one another, like pieces in a jig-saw puzzle; their sensory differences fit together neatly, one zigging where the other zags. The female smells different, looks different, tastes different, and feels different than the male.

You don't need to be an expert to discover if you are strongly attracted to another person. Your attraction to the odor, the look, the taste, the feel of a particular food, for instance, arises on its own from inside you; it is just there, and you can't force it, or create it when it doesn't occur. Sexual attraction works the same way. You may pretend it's there, or ignore its absence, but you pay the price of losing touch with yourself.

Looking, listening, and smelling. These are grouped together because the exercises are similar. Practice concentrating on each of the sensory areas at a different time. Extend these senses to absurd limits. For example, stare at something deliberately until your eyes have absorbed more than you can understand. Listen carefully to sounds, any sound, until it washes out. Smell until you can no longer discover an odor. In each case, search out the smallest detail that you can get from these senses. These can be practiced easily, while waiting for a bus, or standing in a line, or during those long periods when you are waiting for an event or a person.

Talking. Of all the sensory experiences, this is the most integrating for the person. It takes long practice to learn to talk *with your experience* of your inner or outer worlds. The finding of words to fit feelings that arise from sensory awareness, as they occur, is the single most unifying creative act of a human being. The act of finding the words to fit feelings is what organizes you (and everyone) to have an emotional response. When you do each of the above getting-in-touch exercises, practice finding words to fit your feelings *after* they have emerged into your awareness. Wait until you notice a feeling, then *talk with that feeling*, however stupid or random the feeling may seem. Talking with your feelings integrates your inner with your outer world. Practice, practice, practice!

None of these sensory awareness exercises will work successfully for you if you continue to live out of step with simple, unfulfilled needs. If you eat when you're not hungry, if you try to eliminate when you're not ready biologically, if you have sex when you're not strongly attracted to the other person – if you act out of step with any one of these very "close" needs, it will be sufficient to block the healthy dynamic of getting in touch with yourself. Your food, elimination, and sex are especially important because the feedback is direct and instantaneous. This immediately disturbs your contact with yourself and the outer world.

Your *basic needs*, feelings, and emotions are grounded in these areas. Your contact with yourself and the outer world cannot be established successfully until you act in concert with your eating, eliminating, and sexual needs. When this is done, these very close needs subside and are out of the way of your other needs that seek gratification.

Your needs for love, for creative work, and close friends are just as strong as any of the basic needs, but the *priority* is crucial. If a person can't satisfy these most basic needs, he will have great difficulty in recognizing his other needs.

5

Getting in Touch
With Others

Lois was an attractive, dark-haired young woman of twenty-four who felt her life was a disaster. She left home when she was eighteen. After suffering through three attempts to share her apartment with different women of the same age and similar financial circumstances, she decided to live alone. Lois had a job as a secretary with an electronics firm. She wasn't too happy there but she earned an above-average salary and didn't know where or how to improve her salary.

What concerned her most was her failure to find friends, especially men, to share her life with. Every relationship she attempted, with a woman or man, seemed to turn out wrong. She felt she attracted only the worst kind of "loser," persons who took advantage of her, used her badly, and discarded her when she finally cried out and protested against the bad treatment. Her girl friends failed to share the rent as promised, wouldn't cooperate in cooking or cleaning, wouldn't contribute to any of the routine expenses, and seemed to just "step all over her."

Her life with males was no better. Men seemed to take cruel advantage of her. They took her money, her body, and her most tender affections, but treated her with arrogance, as if she didn't deserve any better. And she had come to believe it. She blamed herself for not having the judgment to "see through" people, to know what to expect, so that *she* wouldn't end up a loser, too.

Lois believed people should trust each other, do the right thing, and care for one another, and that if she did this, things would turn out all right. In her most recent affair with a male, she thought matters were going pretty well for a while. She enjoyed sex with him and they seemed to have fun together. Then he introduced her to anal intercourse. It excited and disgusted her, and she worried about her conflicting feelings of enjoyment and self-disgust. She blamed herself for liking what he did. Her worries overshadowed her concern with her friend's sexual behavior. He took her to a party where she discovered he was bisexual, and that he wanted her to take part in sexual activities with the women (and men) in the crowd. This was a crushing blow for Lois, and totally disorganized her. Her tearful complaint was: "My God, where do I go wrong? What's wrong with me that I get all these creeps? I fall in love so easily but always so badly. I must be crazy and need help."

The problem: A lack of roles

Lois couldn't get in touch with other persons, and she literally asked for much of what happened to her. She invited bad treatment and attracted punishment. Lois was out of touch with her outer world of persons, objects, and events. She had only one weak role of social behavior to offer as her personality to others. An anomic personality, she was nearly roleless, and responded too quickly to her feelings. She was bogged down in her inner world. Her single role was "young girl who just left home," and this was the role she played in each encounter with another person.

Lois was probably out of focus to everyone she met. Others couldn't get a clear picture of her because of her lack of personality roles. She gave the impression that she wanted to be submissive and passive, so that the others felt they must respond by dominating her *as if she were* the "young girl who just left home."

If you present yourself in a role, you invite the other person to adopt the role's complement; if you act like a father, you invite someone to assume a son or daughter role. Lois acted like a little girl, so others fell in step and took on a dominating adult role in return.

There are some quick and obvious things that Lois could do by herself to get in touch with others. First, she had to break up her self-defeating role dynamic. Then she had to adopt new roles that fit her needs and the situation. And she had to learn to discard the roles when she no longer felt she needed them.

I should point out that Lois had difficulty striking up friendships. She waited until the other person approached her. Even after an introduction, she was shy and modest, and didn't know how to talk about herself or her interests. Inwardly she believed she was intelligent, and knew more about many things than most of the people she knew. Although her manner did not reflect it, she often felt hostile. Though Lois felt these things, her role of "young girl away from home" required her to be unassuming and nonaggressive. As a result, she attracted verbal personalities who wanted to dominate her.

A program for change

The first step for Lois was to adopt a more aggressive female role for herself. This in itself attracted a different kind of person to her. She bought some chrome-plated letters, and affixed her name, Lois, to the sides and rear of her convertible. Following through, she secured a sticker bearing the name of the firm where she worked, and placed it on the bumper. Of course, she was intelligent enough to realize that she couldn't remake herself overnight and be accepted immediately by persons at the office who were accustomed to her young-woman-away-from-home role. (She planned to do that later.)

Within a week, she hit paydirt with her first new role. As she was driving home from work, a young man pulled alongside her car in the heavy traffic, smiled casually, and followed her car until she turned off on the side street to her apartment. She feared that he would follow her home, but he didn't. Instead, the young man tracked her down by phone the next day and introduced himself. He knew where she worked from the bumper sticker, and he knew her first name from the letters on her car. She turned down his request for a date (as was her strategy). Later she berated herself for not accepting his invitation. However, he called back two days later; this time she agreed to date him. In the meantime, another young man where she worked noticed her car in the parking lot (he worked in a different department and they had never met) and tracked her down too. He came to her desk, introduced himself, and also asked for a date.

Building a new role

Lois worked on another role for herself, one that fitted how she felt about herself. She felt she was pretty, intelligent, and an interesting person, but she was afraid to let others see this side of her. So she took a week's vacation on the coast and built herself a new role. How she did this is important. She did not suddenly try to introduce a new personality to people who were used to her old ways, her old role.

She created a break in the time with a physical absence. Her vacation took her away from persons she knew. In a small coastal town by the beach, she sunned, plotted, and created a role that fit her. She learned a lot about herself very quickly. She met two girls at a beach lunchroom and the three got along immediately. Her two new friends asked her to share their beach cabin and she accepted.

The three got along smoothly, then one of the girls left for home. Within hours, Lois and the other girl had a falling out. Lois suddenly had an insight about her female relationships: A two-person relationship (diad) was disastrous for her. Diads were dangerous, she learned.

The dynamics in the diad (two-person) relationship brought out Lois' need to be dominated by others. She found she reverted to her young-woman-away-from-home role the minute the third girl left the beach cabin. When there were three, Lois didn't tend to seek domination from one or the other, and neither wanted to dominate her. Although one was bossy, the three-person (triad) dynamic prevented domination of one person over another.

The dynamics of the triad

If someone tries to dominate in a triad, he is outnumbered. Two persons must "gang up" on a third to dominate a triad relationship. Nearly always in the diad relationship, however, one person assumes a dominating role.

When Lois returned to her job, she asked two girls *whom she liked* to share her apartment. These two, who were friends, agreed. Lois then had two close female friends, and they got along famously.

Further, when Lois returned from her vacation, she assumed her new role of "I am a pretty, intelligent, and interesting woman." She suffered some fears and guilt about this role, but she persisted. She gained confidence when she saw how differently things went for her with her girl friends, with people at the office, and with her male friends. Everybody she knew had sensed there was more to "Lois" than appeared on the surface. They not only accepted her new version of herself, but expressed their delight, teasing her and encouraging her.

Lois was lucky to have taken this first step so successfully and easily. Generally it takes more hard work and more experimenting for new roles that fit. Lois' next step came much later. She learned how to discard her new role when the occasion was right. In her close relationships with male friends, she learned to use her bright-young-woman role until she was comfortable with a man and knew something about him; then she confided the fears and uncertainties around which she had built her old role.

Lois learned to talk about herself with her feelings, not through the old or new roles. She could control this situation. When she felt she was saying too much, she slipped into her comfortable new role. *She moved from role to rolelessness in a healthy dynamic* that fitted her natural behavior. She had integrated herself. Although she was a more integrated person, she still had tendencies to get out of touch with herself and with others.

Dealing with close relationships

Also important for Lois was the discovery that she could not handle close relationships with more than a few persons at a time. She found that she could be close friends with two girls when altogether they formed a triad relationship. She found she couldn't go out with more than one man at a time if it was to be a deep relationship. Most of these problems of getting in touch with others she learned to handle.

Lois formed casual office relationships, always with two other persons in the group, whether the group was all female or mixed. She didn't try to find "buddies" here and there (to have a lot of scattered diads). Diads, for Lois, as for most anomic persons, were dangerous. They invited authoritarian domination of one person by another.

There was another important integrating role that she adopted. This was a role of "being polite with detached concern" towards persons she didn't like or find attractive. This role kept persons she disliked or feared at a good distance, and fitted alongside her other major role of "bright modern young woman." And both of these roles fit Lois' natural behavior, her tendencies to be under-integrated and out of touch with her outer world. Lois should not have tried to adopt too many different roles. She needed only two or three strong integrating roles that fit her, and could not handle more.

This brings us to some important considerations of the differences in persons, how they get in touch with others, and how they stay in touch. Since Lois had an anomic personality, she should have avoided other persons who had a verbal personality. This was perhaps the most important single lesson for Lois to learn about the personality trap. Being an anomic, Lois could relate only to another anomic person, or to an integrated person. The number of integrated persons is so small, it was best that she not count on meeting one.

Anomic and verbal personalities are so totally at odds in how they relate to their respective inner and outer worlds, I find virtually no successful strong personal relationships between them. The anomic is absorbed and engrossed in his inner world of feelings and emotions and the verbal is embedded in his outer world of objects and external events. The basic personal concerns of these personalities are a million miles apart.

On the battleground of conflicting personalities, the anomic generally is the biggest loser. The verbal inevitably dominates the anomic, but neither finds lasting satisfaction in a relationship with the other. Each is out of touch with the other from the start. One is deeply involved in his inner world (the anomic), and the other is engrossed in the outer world (the verbal). It is a grinding misalliance.

Lois had to learn to spot the verbals and offer them her polite-with-detached-concern role, regardless of how attracted she was to their apparent efficiency and self-control, for the anomic brings out the very worst traits in the verbal personality.

Role dynamics of verbals and anomics

Let me describe once more the contasting role dynamics of these two very different kinds of persons. The anomic is under-integrated in social behavior. He does not make good contact with his outer world nor does he relate well to group ways of doing things. At best, the anomic is able to adopt very few roles that fit him and help him integrate himself.

The anomic absorbes some group ways but does not *project* them into the "personality" he offers in his relationships with others. He does not have a firm, structured personality of roles. The anomic does not *introject* (take in) group ways of doing things intact, that is, without changing them to fit himself. Being unable to introject group ways, "gulp" them down whole, as it were, the anomic then can't *project* them into a "personality" of social behavior.

On the other hand, the verbal personality introjects (takes in whole) without remaking the role, then projects this behavior into a personality for himself. This dynamic is one of the least understood processes in human behavior.

Conventional psychology holds that the verbal personality introjects behavior and then projects his inner world onto the outer world. But this seems an obvious error. The verbal introjects ways of doing things but without assimilating them as his own. Then he projects these introjections into *his own personality of roles,* not to some other person in the outer world. Then the verbal asks persons in the outer world to fit their behavior to his projected personality.

This may seem to be a complex academic argument. I bring it up only to point out the tremendously different amount of energy that is expended by the verbal in maintaining his personality of roles. This constant, unrelieved, unrelenting expenditure of energy needed to bypass his inner world of feelings and emotions creates anxiety which finds expression in feelings of violence toward himself, others, or objects in the outer world.

The "gestalt prayer"

The late Fritz Perls, founder of gestalt therapy, wrote what he called the Gestalt Prayer:

> I do my thing, and you do your thing.
> I am not in this world to live up to
>   your expectations, and you are not
>   in this world to live up to mine.
> You are you, and I am I; if by chance
>   we find each other, it's beautiful.
> If not, it can't be helped.

To me, this is the anomic's prayer for protection from the verbal. Anomics get in touch best only with other anomics, and with integrated persons. The verbal has trouble getting in touch with other verbals, with anomics, or with integrated persons. The verbal is the loneliest human alive. How does the verbal become an integrated person? What does he do to integrate himself, to get in touch with others? Fred is an appropriate example of a verbal.

Fred: A verbal personality

Fred was a man of forty-five who had won honors as an accomplished scientist in the field of physics. He was hand-some, quiet-spoken, respected, and admired for his efficiency in his research and in the organization of his life. Working long hours, he was totally immersed in "selfless" projects related to his field. He taught physics and was known as a tough but fair instructor who got the best out of his students. His course exhausted students but many agreed that they needed his tyranny to pass.

At the university where he taught, or in the industrial laboratory where he worked, other persons saw Fred as one who marched from one place to another engrossed with his thoughts, grim and humorless. Fred seemed to be competent at everything. He was expert with machinery, and with complex ideas, and with organizing, preparing, planning, shaping, and remaking the world around him.

Fred was married to a woman who also had a verbal personality; their life together was nearly a total conflict. Leonore, Fred's wife, was a respected pediatrician, successful and admired. The couple had two children, both anomics, a young man and a young woman.

Fred and Leonore (Lenny) lived in "armed truce" much of the time. They plotted their lives so that they had a weekend now and then to "have it out." These were bitter, brief battles that left surface scars but no deep wounds. They admired each other, and disengaged by means of their you-have-a-right-to-your-opinion-and-I-respect-you-for-it roles.

Although they entered divorce proceedings several times during their twenty-year marriage, each time they "reasoned things through" and were reconciled. They had learned to hate one another with suppressed violence. They also had found ways to express this violence in their brief battles. When they didn't have these encounters, things went very wrong for them; therefore, they had learned to make sure that battles happened from time to time.

The turning point

Both were dispassionate and efficient in their work and in their relationships with other persons, including their children. Fred and Lenny took separate vacations three weeks every year. These were generally expensive trips abroad where they spent all their time with strangers.

Fred started to get in touch with others after a shocking and unexpected event. His daughter Frances was a student away at college. One evening she put on a new party dress, turned on a record of soft music, and swallowed a handful of sleeping pills. She was found dead on her couch.

The sad news of his daughter's suicide crushed Fred. Little by little, he fell apart. The disintegration extended over several days as each surge of feeling built up into an awareness of his inner world. That is, the awareness that he loved another human being (who happened to be his daughter) shattered his personality of roles into fragments. His love for her was intense and penetrating – but it had never been relieved by a show of affection.

His love for Frances had a sexual component that he could not let himself accept as it grew over the years. He had found no way, no role, that would permit him to express his feelings and emotions for her.

The first step for Fred was to realize he should have found a way to respond to his feelings and emotions about Frances, and that this could have been done without having sex with her. Not loving his wife, he fell in love with a young, pretty girl he saw nearly every day – his daughter.

Fred started digging out. To get in touch with others, he began with his family. He didn't like his son; so he finally admitted it and talked it over with him. His son more than understood. He had known for many years that his father didn't care for him, and he was happy to get away from the family to return to college.

Taking another step, Fred divorced Lenny. He gave her their home and moved into a small apartment near his work. Things came slowly to Fred, but he worked them through, making certain he was in touch with how he felt about his actions with others.

Fred realized that he needed organization and structure around him and that he liked to live a formal, impersonal life. This meant he needed to have more formal role relationships with more persons than he did in the past. He wanted an orderly life, one that was well-planned and not plagued with unexpected, spontaneous events. He felt secure in this outer world.

His next move was to join several community organizations. As a member, he met other verbal personalities who liked the same kind of outer world as he did. He could go to meetings and interact with others within their personality of roles, both formal and structured. At the same time, he could get in touch with his inner world. He appreciated this existence.

The outcome

Enjoying life, Fred felt emotional ties with other verbals, and was able to express them from time to time. He found it gratifying to meet with others who shared similar roles of organizational or community goals. He realized that his current experience was vastly different from life with Lenny, a strong verbal personality whom he should never have married.

Fred couldn't stand to be with anomics, but he needed to be very careful about the verbals he associated with, too. Two strong verbal personalities cannot get in touch with one another very easily. It was possible that Fred would be able to find a "softer" verbal woman who would fit him rather well.

Examples reveal basic steps

Hopefully, the examples of Lois and Fred clearly reveal the basic steps required for getting in touch with others. For example, both Lois and Fred first had to get in touch with themselves, to understand what their fundamental and primary needs were, and whether they could share both their inner or outer worlds.

In the earlier example, Lois came to see that she was more engrossed with her inner life of feelings and emotions, and less concerned about the outer world of things and events. The outer world interested her, but she was secure only when her inner world was "right." As for Fred, he came to realize that his primary interest was in the outer world of doing things, of manipulating objects and persons, of changing the world around him to fit his ideals. He was secure only when his outer world was "right," with things and persons neatly in place.

Both Fred and Lois believed that they had a mixture of anomic and verbal traits. As they grew closer in touch with themselves — Lois to experience her outer world more, and Fred to get the feel of his inner world better — the feeling of being a mixture became stronger. This meant they were getting more in touch with their natural behavior.

The main guideline for each remained the same as before: Lois could get out of touch with her outer world and still feel healthy as long as she had love or affection with one, two, or perhaps three other persons in a close relationship. Fred could drift out of touch with his inner world and remain healthy as long as he was involved in his outer world of well-organized, structured existence. If they lost touch with the world wherein they had their deepest anchors (inner world for Lois and outer for Fred), they started getting out of touch with other persons.

From time to time they would think things through a-
gain, to rediscover their basic needs, to get in contact with
themselves, and to make corrections if some were needed.
They became *self-regulating persons.* They integrated
their natural and social behavior. They were able to choose
roles that fit them (that fit their basic needs), roles that allowed them to get in touch with others and to satisfy their personal ways of doing things at the same time. Both learned to
adjust their roles to fit themselves. They did not try to adjust to fit some role, some way of doing things that was contrary to their nature. Nor did they associate with persons they
had to adjust themselves to.

By finding persons who fit them from the start, they
avoided the personality trap in which someone had to change
to fit the other. Both Fred and Lois realized it was much easier
to find persons who fit them than it was to get people to
change. Getting people to change was difficult and a great
waste of time!

Integration achieved

To repeat: Fred and Lois became integrated persons.
They stayed in touch with others because they learned how
to get in touch with themselves; this enabled them to know
what kind of persons they needed to get in touch with.

Fred continued to teach at a college because he liked the
formal roles and the transmission of objective facts and information. He liked to associate with students and other
teachers on an impersonal basis. He resigned from his job
with the industrial firm for he decided he didn't like working
alone in a small lab. He got another position with a larger
firm where he had charge of the lab with several persons
under him. He enjoyed the structured contact in a chain of
command, the responsibility, and having persons both superior and subordinate to him. He was anchored in his outer
world with these relationships. When these relationships
were "right," Fred got in touch with his inner feelings and
emotions.

As for Lois, it didn't make much difference to her what kind of a job she had. Having a few close personal friends who cared about her at her job was what counted. More importantly, Lois fell in love and was loved in return by a young man who fitted her. She couldn't have cared less about what happened in her outer world as long as she had a tight little cluster of persons—in this case, her lover and friends. She didn't seek many friendships or more than one lover—nor could she handle more. But she made certain that the persons she chose fit her.

Don't try to change others — let them be!

She didn't get involved with those who had to change in order for her to be satisfied with them. This is a difficult lesson for many people to learn, and it didn't come easily for Fred or Lois. Once they learned where their primary needs were, they could recognize similar persons fairly easily. A person cannot change his primary orientation as an inner world or outer world anchored individual.

What Fred and Lois learned to do was to recognize these basically different kinds of persons and to avoid those who didn't fit. When for some reason they were thrown together with people who didn't fit them, they had roles to use for protection and social distance. Fred liked to be with large groups of persons at work or play or at home. Lois liked small, two-or-three person groups, wherever she was.

Being integrated persons, they were fair, honest, and cooperative in their dealings with others. They didn't try to change persons who didn't fit them. *They let them be.* They avoided them when possible and tried to make contact only with those who shared similar personal needs. Fred thrived on role talk, talk about talk, talk-talk with others, and acting in his many different roles. Lois thrived on touch, laughter, crying, kissing, hugging, love, and sex. She had only two strong roles: She chattered like a chipmunk when relating to a close friend or lover, but with others, she had little to say.

She got "lost" in crowds, so avoided them. She had "lost" feelings when she was not near someone who cared for her, and for whom she cared in return.

Both Fred and Lois integrated themselves and got in touch with others. They found basic integrating roles that fit their natural behavior. Fred may seem to be a "strong" personality and Lois a "weak" personality. But in reality, they were both whole persons who learned what to do to get in touch with themselves and others.

6

How to Start Your
Own Gestalt Group

Bryan was a college student in his senior year. He was an education major and intended to teach high school math as a career. During his years in college, he worked part-time, sometimes full time, to pay his way through. He roomed with his mother and stepfather, but seldom saw either of them. He stayed out of their way as much as possible. Bryan entered college to avoid the draft. When, at age nineteen, he changed his mind and tried to enlist, he flunked his physical. Later, at twenty-one, Bryan was enthusiastic about becoming a math teacher. But that was his *only* joy. He had no friends, male or female. He worked or studied most of the time, and he felt that he was quietly and slowly going crazy.

He awoke every morning depressed with himself and his life. It became more and more difficult for him to get his work done either at school or at his job. He daydreamed a lot about his future, and spun elaborate sexual fantasies. As time went on, he found he spent increasing amounts of time with these daydreams, drifting away from the work at hand. He had had one incomplete sexual experience with a girl, in which he failed; he reworked this failure in fantasy, time and again. He relied on masturbation usually once in the morning and again in the evening, in his room at home, for relief.

You no doubt are aware that Bryan created an anomic personality for himself. He was out of touch with himself and with others. He had very few roles, none of which fit him, and was under-integrated in his social behavior. He was too close to his inner world of feelings and emotions, and felt out of place in his outer world of jobs, persons, and things he came in contact with daily. He was bored with his job, didn't care about having his old car fixed when it broke down, and didn't know how to talk to people when he met them. He was shy with both males and females.

Working alone or with others

Bryan began working at getting in touch with himself by means of the sensory awareness exercises. Enthusiastically, he worked his way through breathing, eating, envisioning, bathing, talking out loud, smelling, touching, seeing, hearing, and others that he invented. Nothing seemed to work well for him, if indeed at all.

He found that bathing in the tub, for instance, ended in masturbation, which he felt was not the intent of the exercise. He was encouraged to set aside most of the sensory awareness work with himself for a while and concentrate on getting in touch with his outer world. Later he could return to getting in touch with his inner world. This meant that he would do his getting-in-touch work when he was with other persons, and not do the exercises when he was by himself.

Frequently, this is the best (and only) way an anomic personality can get in touch with himself or others. And the opposite seems to be true for the verbal personality. The verbal should concentrate on the "close" sensory awareness exercises in eating, breathing, listening, seeing, touching, talking out loud, bathing, and especially envisioning, when by himself. The verbal is out of touch with his inner world and needs to work on how he experiences feelings and emotions. Then he can move on to linking these with his feelings and emotions, his inner life. Whether verbal or anomic, an individual needs to include other persons soon after starting the exercises if he hopes to integrate himself. This means learning how to start a gestalt group.

A young male student in one of the classes had spoken out several times during lectures and Bryan was impressed with his coolness and ability to speak. Bryan, who remained silent in class, usually sat in the back row near the door, a little apart from the others. Les, the student Bryan was impressed with, sat in the back row too, but it didn't seem to matter because he spoke loudly and confidently, and everybody heard him. Bryan liked Les' ideas, so he asked him to have some coffee with him after class one day.

Bryan also had his eye on a coed, Jeanette, in another class. Although she, too, was the silent type in class, he liked her black hair, quietness, and femininity. He invited both her and Les to come to his home for refreshments and to listen to some new records. He added that he wanted them to meet a few of his friends—whom he invented on the spur of the moment. To his surprise, the pair agreed to come. Of course, then Bryan had to round up other acquaintances.

Bryan phoned an old friend, Mac, whom he hadn't seen since high school, and invited him to come over and meet Les and Jeanette. Mac agreed (apparently pleased) and asked if it would be all right to bring along his girl of some two years. Reluctantly, Bryan included Mac's girl, Cheryl, in the invitation. The gathering was set for a Friday. Bryan had the house to himself for the weekend.

Bryan had created a "loose" gestalt group for himself. First, Bryan knew (to some degree) and liked all of the persons he had invited except for Mac's girl. And Mac almost certainly liked his own girl, so this seemed a positive factor. Everyone invited knew at least one other person in the group. This comprised a "loose" gestalt because Bryan was the central bond drawing the group together, and the others didn't know each other.

A more important factor is that *Bryan chose persons he was attracted to;* he did not choose them because he knew them well or because they knew each other, although these were considerations. His group was a natural group, a gestalt group that emerged from his network of associations with other persons. Gestalt groups, in my definition, are any natural small group of persons that include from two to five members. Bryan's group had a total of five persons, and was formed from diad bonds between himself and Les, Jeanette, and Mac, and Mac and his girl.

Group size is important

The most effective "new" gestalt group seems to be a five-person group, or *quin*, of mixed sex. Two-, three-, or four-person gestalt groups have much different group dynamics than the quin. New groups larger than five seldom work out. Even in old groups larger than five, people have difficulties relating to one another person-to-person, outside their roles of personality.

It is doubtful that an evening with just Bryan and Les and Jeanette would have come off well (although the triad, or three-person group, produces one of the better gestalts). For now, let's see what happened with Bryan's quin. Each person of the group spent the first hour or so acting within his or her personality of roles. Everyone liked Mac's girl, Cheryl, right off; and Cheryl took to Bryan, much to his embarrassment. Bryan and Mac discovered they still liked each other, perhaps more so than before. And Les took immediately to Jeanette.

Bryan didn't like some of these "dynamics" but restrained his first inner response (an anomic usually tends to respond too soon, too quickly to inner feelings) and kept himself "loose." During an awkward silence, Bryan blurted out his reasons for getting the group together. To his surprise, the others seemed pleased and interested in what he was trying to do with himself.

Bryan described his attempts to get in touch with himself and how they had failed. He did not go into his fears and feelings of guilt, just that he was "up tight" and wanted to "get right" with himself. This worked its way into his specific problems later, quite naturally. Bryan had never been able to talk about himself in a personal way before.

Bryan's group established some practical ground rules for themselves the first evening. To begin with, they agreed that Bryan's home wasn't suitable for the group. They agreed to move their meetings to Mac's apartment which offered plenty of chairs, easy access to kitchen and bathroom, and especially, it offered privacy. Mac lived alone so they would not be interrupted by persons not involved in the group. This was very important. At Bryan's home, his mother or step-father might walk in and out of the room and disturb the feeling of privacy.

Next, the group decided to meet regularly on Friday evenings for at least three hours. If a person missed more than one meeting, he would have to drop out of the group. If two persons could not make a meeting, the meeting would be put off until another time. These were necessary ground rules. If the group wasn't involved and committed to at least regular weekly meetings of three hours, nothing much could happen; that is, it hasn't time to happen.

The group agreed that anything that came up during meetings would be kept absolutely confidential; that nothing that was said or done, no matter how trivial it seemed, would be discussed with anyone who was not in the group. They agreed that it was part of their purpose for members to discuss things among themselves after meetings, but not with outsiders.

Shortly after the first meeting started, the group decided that there would be no formal leader. Bryan acted as host, but Mac, Les, and Cheryl tended to "take over" from time to time. All soon saw that no one person should dominate the group. At any given time leadership during a session should emerge with the situation as when one person wanted to try something out or suggest something for others in the group. The group learned quickly that "dead silence" was not really awkward, but was in fact good to have now and then because it allowed time to mull things over.

One of the more important decisions made the first night was to develop an agenda, a loose structure or guide to follow, of things the group wanted to do, and to try out with each other and themselves. The following is a part of the group rules and agenda developed by Bryan's group:

1. Every event or thought must be discussed *in the present*. Group members may talk only about how they feel *now* about an event or their feelings or responses. Persons may talk about what they did yesterday or last month if they speak about how they feel *now* about the event. (This ground rule really means not to talk about the past or the future except as either may be integrated with a present experience.)

2. Meetings will be started with each group member giving his present feelings about every other group member. (This seems to get the group anchored in the present.)

3. Each person will describe what he feels is his worst personal trait, his greatest weakness.

4. Each person will describe what he feels is his strongest personal trait, his best characteristic.

5. Each person will choose the person in the group he likes the best, and tell why. Then he will choose the person he likes the least, and tell why.

6. Each person will describe what he feels are the worst and best acts he committed in his life, and why he feels the acts were the worst and best.

7. Each person will describe the most nagging worry in his life.

8. Each person will describe in detail the most pleasurable moment in his life.

9. Each person will describe in detail his favorite daydream.

10. Each person will choose his favorite fantasy and build it to include one other person from the group.

All of the persons in Bryan's group had to learn something very difficult: How to talk in the present *with their feelings* as these feelings occur. Bryan, Jeanette, and to a lesser degree, Cheryl, did not know how to express themselves well verbally, to find words to fit their inner world of feelings and emotions. These three had anomic personalities, and talking out loud about how they felt was difficult.

Les and Mac, verbal personalities, had a different set of problems. They talked easily and had plenty of words to use, but they had trouble getting in touch with their inner world of feelings. Les and Mac were quick to say what they thought they should say, but were out of touch with how they really felt and with what was going on inside them.

Some examples from agenda items 1 and 2

The anomics (Bryan, Jeanette, and Cheryl) had to learn to find words that fit their feelings; and the verbals, Mac and Les, had to learn to notice what their feelings were, then use words that fit them. For example, Bryan liked both Jeanette and Cheryl on first sight. He sat across from Jeanette in one group session and described what he felt about her at the moment:

"I sure do like your eyes, their blue color, your pupils — they seem to dance. I like your hair. It reminds me now of black softness, something soft to touch . . . I feel uneasy, frightened, saying that to you . . . I shouldn't have said it . . . but I'm glad I did . . . I like your height. I'm taller than you . . . you have a funny laugh sometimes . . . I wonder what it's like to kiss you . . . I don't like saying that either but I do like it . . . I don't want to offend you . . . ."

Bryan shifted to Cheryl, and discovered something about how he felt: "I like you too, Cheryl, very much . . . I'm a little scared of you for some reason . . . you seem to be laughing at me inside . . . I want you to touch me . . . touch my face . . . I want to feel your hands . . . I like you better than Jeanette, better than anyone here, except maybe Mac, even Mac I guess, I don't care about Mac right now . . . just how I'm sounding, coming off . . . it's important to me, for you to like me . . . ."

And, on Mac's turn: "I'm glad you invited me here, Bryan. I'm not all that glad . . . I figured I'd get bored . . . I remember you as pretty dull . . . that's not fair . . . I don't feel that now . . . I don't like you going for Cheryl . . . but . . . I don't like Cheryl going for you even more . . . you always wanted my girl friends in school and couldn't get them . . . now you are paying me back . . . that's a kick . . . who the hell do you think you are?"

These kind of expressions would be unusual in an early meeting. Generally it takes some time for most people to learn to *notice* what's going on in their inner world, and to find the words that fit the emerging feelings, to *speak with their experience of another person.* Inner feelings are so vague and nearly always so personal that they are often excluded from verbal expression. Mac finally learned by expressing himself verbally to objects rather than to persons. He would pick up a pillow and "talk with his feelings" about the way the pillow may have been used up to the present, and how he could use it now.

Speaking integrates experiences

Verbals, like Mac and Les, can talk easily about things, about ideas or events in their outer world. But they have difficulty describing how they feel inside about their outer world of persons or events. Verbals are out of touch with their inner world of feelings and emotions. Anomics are out of touch with their outer world; they have difficulty finding words to fit their feelings about persons or objects outside. Both the verbal and the anomic link their inner and outer worlds when they find words to fit their inner feelings and express these words out loud. The act of speaking with their experience in the present *integrates* their inner and outer experiences.

When either the verbal or anomic gets involved in this dynamic, he begins to integrate himself, and the more it is practiced, the quicker the integration. It is important to do this with other persons, but it seems to be beneficial when done with objects or things, too.

Agenda items 3 and 4

Cheryl described her worst personal trait, or weakness: "I never finish anything . . . I'm unreliable . . . I lie all the time about how I feel . . . I guess that's the worst . . . I lie to my mother . . . to Mac . . . I'm lying to all of you now . . . my worst trait, I feel, is I can't say no . . . I'm too promiscuous . . . always have been . . . anyone can screw me . . . I like it too much sometimes . . . I'm not much good . . . all a boy has to do is touch me between the legs and I'm gone . . . I'm a nymphomaniac 'cause I don't even like most men and I know I would screw anyone and this makes me sick with myself . . . ."

Cheryl described her strongest personal trait, her best characteristic: "I'm generous, friendly with everyone, I listen . . . want to listen to anyone's problems . . . I'll give away my clothes even . . . I always try to help others . . . I have lots of friends who talk over their deep secrets with me, confide in me and trust me . . . ."

Agenda item 5

Mac described the person he liked best in the group, then the one he liked the least: "Les. I like you the best now, I like the way you handle yourself . . . I like your shoes . . . you don't say too much but you know what you're talking about I think . . . I like your car . . . I like your movements with yourself . . . I don't really know too much about you . . . I don't like you, Jeanette, you seem phony . . . that smile is crappy . . . why don't you say what's on your mind? . . . you're too quiet . . . always thinking or maybe just blank, not thinking at all . . . you haven't said one single word that's sharp. I don't like the way you dress . . . ."

Agenda item 6

Bryan described what he felt was the single worst act he ever committed, and then his best act: "This is hard for me . . .

I've never told anyone about this . . . my God, this is rough . . . I jacked-off my dog when I was about fourteen . . . but there's more . . . I jacked him off then I jacked-off and that dog licked it off . . . and I did this twice in a week when I was sleeping out on the back porch and then I moved back into the house even though it was hot as hell . . . .

"This one seems hard . . . I can't think of a best thing I have done . . . I guess . . . maybe I feel the best is when I knew my dad was running around with some girl and I saw him . . . no, someone told me they saw him . . . and I didn't tell mom . . . ."

Agenda item 7

Les described the most nagging worry in his life: "I guess my family bothers me the most . . . my dad's a real shit and mother just goes along with him although she suffers like hell with his temper and sometimes beatings . . . I don't understand her . . . why she puts up with him . . . he can knock her around and the next minute she's cooking his dinner as if nothing happened . . . this just tears me up . . . two years ago he beat her up then slapped me around too and I went and got my rifle and he didn't believe I meant it until he saw me put a shell in the gun and cock it . . . then he turned white . . . I was ready to kill him and he knew it . . . I didn't say any more . . . I just put the gun down and walked out . . . and I've never been back . . . I learned something then . . . to get away from people I don't like . . . to stay away when I see I can't stand them . . . to get off on my own and live by myself as I do now and choose just those people I can get along with and who can get along with me . . . everything else is bullshit . . . but this causes me trouble . . . I can't stay with a job too long . . . I get a dead feeling a lot . . . and the only thing I really care about is my car . . . ."

Agenda item 8

Jeanette described the most pleasurable moment in her life: "I don't know how to talk about this . . . it's real weird . . .

and it's still true . . . when I was a little girl I used to go to the park next door to us . . . after dark, only when it was dark . . . and swing in the swing there . . . I would swing until my arms ached and my back hurt . . . mom and dad would always be upset with me . . . punish me . . . but I still like to do this . . . it may be something sexual but it's far more than just that, I know it is . . . in the night I seem to fly and be free, and God what a feeling . . . I try not to do it too much . . . especially now that the parks are so bad at night . . . I haven't gone now in years . . . ."

Agenda item 9

Cheryl described her favorite daydream: "Well, this sounds like a broken record playing the same old thing you've all heard . . . sex . . . I'm sex crazy . . . it's always the same daydream . . . just variations . . . variety . . . I'm a high priestess dressed in flowing see-through robes with several naked men each bringing me gifts, attending to my every little need . . . it's all so elaborate . . . they always rub me with oil all over first, bathe me with soft sponges then carefully oil me all over again slowly . . . there's soft religious music playing . . . then there's just three men I've picked out . . . I'm kind of tied to a gold stake . . . a sacrifice, a high priestess duty I have to do . . . and then we all slowly come together and the men all scream with pleasure . . . ."

Agenda item 10

Bryan described his favorite fantasy, and constructed the fantasy to include Jeanette: "I remember your talking about swinging at night, in the darkness, and that really means something to me . . . at the time I felt just like I was there with you . . . but not really with you exactly, but inside you somehow . . . swinging with you, feeling your feelings too . . . when you felt them I felt them too . . . when you feel them I feel them too, keeping in the present . . . I see us on a carpet at night above the clouds . . . I'm still inside of you, bodiless, just an ectoplasm or a ghost . . . there are colors, slow blue colors, but it's also dark and we sleep together . . . high above the world and free . . . ."

The ten agenda items were worked through fairly quickly in Bryan's group. The group added others when they wanted to move on to something different. They combined some items and developed new ones. For example:

Additional agenda items

Recalling unpleasant memories or nightmares. This became one of the more productive experiences for this group. Each member would sit back and let the feelings of the moment about an unpleasant recent experience emerge to awareness, on their own thrust. Sometimes they would use unpleasant night dreams in the same manner, as follows:

Mac spoke: "I can't get over your going for Bryan, Cheryl . . . it bugs me for some reason . . . I'm looking at you now and I don't feel anything . . . I know you're an easy lay but I didn't think I minded . . . but something bugs me about this . . . Bryan, Bryan bugs me . . . it makes me angry to think you like Bryan better than me . . . what's Bryan got that I don't . . . I think he's a slob in some ways . . . I like Bryan a little . . . but not much . . . what is it about you Bryan . . . you know by God I think you are a good-looking man . . . that's it! . . . I think you're better looking than me . . . always have, I guess . . . you look too pretty . . . my hands are always dirty and yours are always clean . . . like you never work . . . never had to work . . . why should Cheryl like you when you probably couldn't satisfy her like I can . . . but maybe I'm afraid you could and be prettier than me at the same time . . . ."

Sensory awareness exercises. This item included a variety of experiments listed earlier for getting in touch with oneself. Bryan's group experimented with those they could do together.

The group eventually started their sessions with eating together. They ordered a variety of foods so that each had some he liked best. Members of the group ate chicken, steak, Chinese food, and pizza. They deliberately experienced the food in different ways. Each would silently notice what he was experiencing in the way of appearance, then taste, then after-taste, then talk with his experience as he continued to eat. They would not talk to one another, except about what they were feeling about their food, then, at the moment.

Les talked: "This piece of steak doesn't look as good as the one just before . . . it's too red inside . . . I like the done part better . . . I think I will squash this . . . I am squashing it . . . it feels good . . . now it doesn't . . . in fact I won't eat this piece of crap . . . I don't like the bread with this tonight . . . Jeanette, your pizza looks better than this steak . . . I guess I like watching you eat it anyway . . . you seem to enjoy the hell out of it . . . you seem real sexy eating pizza . . . how do you feel eating pizza?"

These awareness experiments also included touch contact. Someone would hold another's hand and talk about how he was experiencing the other person. Or, they would ponder what part of the other person was most attractive and tell why this was true. They listened to each other's breathing; they shut their eyes and listened to the sound of their voices; and they also tried to identify each other (eyes still closed) by smell.

Achievements of the group

There were two major achievements that group members came to, each in his own way and at different times over the first few months. First, each learned to express himself verbally out loud, to talk with his inner feelings, to find words to fit what was going on inside.

The second was that each became aware that he didn't need to pretend to like someone that he didn't find attractive. This included an understanding that they really didn't like someone if they wanted that person to change as a condition of the relationship. This seemed very important. Mac discovered, for instance, that he really wanted Cheryl to change, to be another kind of girl, that he really didn't care for her as a person the way she was.

He realized it was easier to find a girl who already fit his ideal and who didn't have to change to become something he wanted. This discovery was a key to the success of the group. They found that they could not relate to one another within their personalities, their roles, and their expectations of one another. They found that they could care for one another, in different degrees, when they responded to each other outside their role behavior.

These understandings did not come easily and occurred over many months, (including the time lost by meetings that were called off). But the group was held together by a number of different kinds of bonds. Some friendships were formed and some deeper attachments grew.

Let me point out some of the things that happened to help this gestalt group become successful. First, the group was a natural gestalt. Each person knew someone else as a result of coming in contact with one another; the group members selected themselves. Participation in the group was voluntary. While each one was chosen by someone else to come in, the chosen one, in turn, chose to enter.

A gestalt group is not a therapy group. Bryan's group did not come together to have "therapy," but to develop relationships responsive to deep personal needs. This made the group a natural one, and not an artificial group where persons come together and interact with one another in their personalities of roles. No one in Bryan's group was mentally ill; they were all "normal" persons.

This first step, one of getting together for the right reasons and forming a natural, not an artificial, group is the most significant problem to overcome. Although Bryan and the others came together within their personalities of roles at first, their main purpose was to find others who "fit" their personal needs. They learned to discard their personality of roles.

Next, they chose a private, comfortable, easy-to-reach place to meet regularly, and established a sense of trust and confidence by agreeing that these meetings were personal and not to be shared with anyone outside the group. The meetings were held indoors, not outdoors where distractions from the outside world would interfere.

The problem of leadership

The group then dealt with the problem of leadership. The members recognized that no one person would be the "leader," that leadership must be shared. Sometimes one, sometimes another would come forward as a guide toward something he or she felt was worthwhile for himself. They realized that disaster resulted when one group member attempted to dominate or impose a problem or task on the others. They made room for *self-concern* as the meetings progressed, and as this emerged from time to time with different members, it became the leadership. This "leadership of self-concern" became more evident as individuals gained confidence in expressing how they felt and began to trust their own feelings and responses.

As this pattern of leadership emerged, it was shared fairly equally. It shifted in a flowing, free-form way as persons moved in to lead for awhile in the interest of their own self-concern, then surrendered the lead when the concern was satisfied and the focus rotated to another person. These unintended directions, unplanned and free flowing, are imperative to good gestalt. This is something each group has to allow to develop, and will do so with experience.

There is a difference between leadership and petty dominance, however. All groups struggle with this. Verbals tend to dominate small groups, and others get bored with their problems. Verbals (and sometimes anomics) tend to take protracted side trips, to get caught up in some event outside the concern of the group. When this happened in Bryan's group, they learned to "shut off" the person's flow. Bryan's group agreed from the start that when these side trips occurred—when a member began talking about himself or about events outside what was going on with persons in the group—any other group member could ask for a change in discussion. This one agreement kept the group from getting bogged down.

The group learned that the best ground rule is to talk only about how you feel *about yourself or about another person* in that group. One had to stay current, in the present, and not dwell on what happened last year or yesterday. They learned that persons adopt role behavior and assume their personalities whenever they drift into the past or the future in their thinking.

They learned to preface their remarks with, "I believe now," "I feel," "I think," "I am," "Right now I bet," and so on, to anchor their verbal expression with the present emerging inner feeling or response. Rolelessness is always in the present; a creative act is always in the present.

The group noticed that persons tend to lecture one another, or speak in generalities: One time Mac said, "I think most people in the world really want to be kind to one another." This was a lecture. He should have said, for good gestalt, "I want to be kind to other people. I want other people to be kind to me." This lecturing, this verbal diarrhea, is role talk, talk-talk, talk about talk, and not a felt experience by Mac or anyone trying to *hear* him. The group worked on Les and Mac to curb their "lecturing" tendencies.

Play and roleless behavior

Another important thing the group learned was that roleless behavior (acting outside their personalities) was enhanced with play. Play behavior is roleless when a person becomes absorbed in the play. Bryan's group learned how to be absurd without embarrassment, to joke with humor, to be playful with one another. Jeanette, for example, didn't think she liked to be touched. She discovered that she liked very much to have her toes fondled. Once she had her shoes off and Les playfully and gently twisted her toes.

Creative behavior is roleless behavior, and play behavior is one form of both. Jeanette couldn't retain her "quiet girl" role when she started laughing and enjoying something as simple as her toes being fondled. Eventually, no one was surprised by the wealth of emotion and expression that existed in them, somewhere below the surface of their awareness. Tears, crying, laughing, giggles, anger, pouting, pleasure — all appeared when the path was opened in an atmosphere of caring for one another as persons, not as personalities.

Another important point learned in Bryan's group was that each group (and member) discovers its own special ways of doing things. Much happens without individuals trying to make things happen.

A review of group rules

Let's review briefly the ground rules developed by Bryan's group:

Each person discards roles or social scripts on how to behave, and strives for rolelessness in how he relates to others.

Each person stays current — in the present — when he talks *with* his feelings, not about them.

Each person talks only in the present, not about past or future events. Feelings exist only in the present.

Leadership is shared. Decisions are made by the group on when and where to meet, and what to do.

Once going, if a member doesn't want to meet, the group cancels the meeting. Continued absence warns the group that it may be time to disband. This rule should be strictly observed.

Once disbanded, a new gestalt group may be formed in the same manner as the first. But new members cannot replace someone who has dropped out. It is better to dissolve the group. It is very difficult to "catch up" a replacement as this generally leads to artificial relationships.

When someone leaves the group and another person is added, it is to be treated as a new group. The gestalt changes completely.

In the next chapter, I will examine the small group dynamics of Bryan's group — what goes on in gestalt groups.

7

What Goes On in Gestalt Groups

The gestalt group of Bryan, Les, Mac, Jeanette, and Cheryl turned out well in many different ways. The psychodynamics behind the relationships are worth noting carefully. Bryan and the two girls, Jeanette and Cheryl, had anomic personalities. They made up a triad, and formed closer bonds with each other (became better friends) than they did with Les or Mac. Bryan and Cheryl fell in love; Jeanette and Cheryl remained good friends.

Les and Jeanette became lovers. Mac and Les became good friends. (Mac and Les were both verbals.) Mac lost a girl friend, but gained a close male friend. Mac was tired of Cheryl it seemed, anyway. The dynamics of all this occurred over a period of many weeks, but followed the paths of attraction established by the first impressions each had of the other, which they revealed and talked about in one of the group exercises.

Bryan still liked Jeanette, but he liked Cheryl more. Both had anomic personalities, but Cheryl was a *more aggressive anomic* than Jeanette, and fitted Bryan better. Les was a strong verbal and got along well with a soft verbal such as Mac. Also, quiet anomics like Jeanette are attracted to strong verbals such as Les. This Les-Jeanette (strong verbal and quiet anomic) combination occurs frequently, but the relationships are not too satisfactory.

Probably Les and Jeanette would split up later. The bonds that had the best chance to endure were the ones between Les and Mac (verbals), Bryan and Cheryl (anomics), and Cheryl and Jeanette (anomics). Bryan, Cheryl, and Jeanette had a triad bond also.

Verbals and anomics are not abnormal

The preceding experiences point up the importance of an individual able to recognize what kind of person he is, and what kind of persons others are, when starting his own gestalt groups. Just how to do it is the dilemma. First of all, remember that I use the terms "anomic" and "verbal" to describe *normal* human behavior tendencies. No one in Bryan's quin was sick, or "abnormal." If someone has created an extremely anomic personality for himself, he would fall into the conventional psychology category of "neurotic," or "psychoneurotic." An extremely verbal personality would be classified in conventional terms as a "psychotic."

Let's examine the lines of attraction between persons in Bryan's group. Anomics, like Bryan, are attracted to other anomics, like Jeanette and Cheryl, since they understand and communicate well with each other. They are more caught up in their inner world of feelings and emotions, and do not understand or do well with things or events in the outer world. So, there is a natural attraction among anomics Bryan, Jeanette, and Cheryl.

Cheryl was a very aggressive anomic whereas Bryan was not so aggressive. Bryan, then, was drawn more to Cheryl than to Jeanette, although he liked Jeanette, too. But the deeper bond developed between Bryan and aggressive Cheryl; they "fit" one another in a more complementary, jigsaw-puzzle manner.

Anomics are also attracted to verbals, but for different reasons. While anomic Bryan communicated with and understood other anomics well, he was attracted to verbal persons who seemed to know how to cope with the outer world. For instance, Jeanette, an anomic, was strongly attracted to verbal Les, who was self-confident, did things well, and so on. Jeanette needed and wanted someone who would teach her how to do things, and how to cope with her outer world. She wanted to learn ways to deal with other persons, to get jobs, to satisfy her personal needs – the things she had not been able to do.

So, she was attracted to Les, not because she understood him but because she needed him to help her cope with her outer world. Verbals Les and Mac, in turn, were attracted to anomics because anomics seem to be in close touch with their feelings and emotions. The verbal is out of touch with his inner world of feelings and emotions and is drawn to the anomic in the hope that the latter can help him discover this inner experience. But the closest relationship a verbal can have is with another verbal because they understand one another. Both are engrossed more in their outer than in their inner worlds. Like the anomics, the verbals communicate better with one another.

Anomics and verbals form limited relationships with each other

Although verbals and anomics form relationships with one another, the *depth* of the relationship is limited because of the difference in their relationship with the outer world (and inner world). Verbals and anomics can learn from one another, but the relationship will be limited. Discontent seems inevitable when they reach out for very personal, deep communication to get in touch with one another. Their views of the world are from opposite sides: one from inner feelings and emotions, the other from how things exist outside in the external world.

If anomic Jeanette and verbal Les found each other attractive enough to get married, the marriage would most likely bring discontent for both very quickly, and this discontent would probably continue throughout their years together. Jeanette would be less discontented with Bryan, but being nonaggressive anomics, they would be two slender reeds leaning on each other in a strong wind, barely managing to stay halfway upright.

If Jeanette and Bryan married, they probably would not acquire much material security, such as the right jobs, a nice home, a financially comfortable life. This could lead to unhappiness for both. Bryan seemed much better off with an aggressive anomic such as Cheryl – aggressive in the sense that she accepted her "disorganization" and tendency to fall apart, and she knew she had to work to get things done. In short, she didn't mind being anomic. She accepted and liked herself, and did the things she had to do to find persons and things that fit her natural behavior. Cheryl had fears and guilt, and continued to blame herself for the way she was, but she accepted the fact that this was the way she was.

Cheryl laughed a lot, had a broad sense of humor, and found enjoyment in little or big things. She had a silly playful streak, and verbal Mac and Les, and anomic Bryan and Jeanette were drawn to her immediately. Mac didn't quite know why she bored him, nor why he didn't mind when Cheryl dropped him for Bryan. But Cheryl sensed the fit between herself and Bryan, and aggressively pushed the relationship.

The way a person talks is a clue to his personality

A direct clue to whether someone tends to have a verbal or anomic personality is in the way he talks. Each member of Bryan's group listened carefully to what one another said. Verbals tend to refer to outside events when talking about themselves or happenings. For instance, verbals Les and Mac almost always referred to things or persons acting on them. Mac said: "Les' idea hits me as right . . . Everybody seems to like wine, and I do too . . . No one else seems to like wine, but I do . . . Everybody is growing their hair long, but I'm keeping mine short . . . . Jeanette makes me feel good . . . .

Cheryl sure livens up my life . . . . Bryan's quietness bugs me
. . . . That lamp shines in my eyes."

Also, verbals tend to use the "it" term: "It seems to me,"
"It occurs to me," "It may not be true but," "It should make
you happy that I care for you."

In their talk, verbals Les and Mac referred to events, persons, or objects in their outside world (either as "it" or by
naming the reference group or event: "everyone," "everybody," "no one," "most persons I know," etc.) as responsible
for their personal reactions. That is the way the verbal views
the world. His inner reactions are guided and determined by
what's happening outside and how it's acting on him. The
anomics are just the opposite in the way they talk (unless they
are trying to mimic the verbal way).

Anomics Bryan, Jeanette, and Cheryl found that when
talking they tended to put their point of reference inside
themselves: "I'm bothered by that light," not "That light
bothers me," as a verbal might say; "I feel sorry for Bryan,"
not "Bryan makes me feel sorry for him," as a verbal might
say; "I feel uncomfortable in this chair," not "This chair
hurts my back."

The differences between the anomic and verbal personalities nearly always can be determined from the way they talk
about their respective worlds:

Verbals (Les and Mac)	*Anomics* (Bryan, Jeanette, and Cheryl)
This group sure turns me on.	*I* sure am turned on in this group.
Bryan's silence bugs me.	*I am bothered* when Bryan is silent.
That dog's yapping makes me sick.	*I get sick* when that dog yaps.
Cheryl's laugh makes me happy.	*I laugh* when Cheryl laughs.
That fork may hurt me.	*Don't hurt me* with that fork.
You sure scare me.	*I'm scared* by you.

The spoken reference usually is clear; the verbal's outer world is where he lives, and the anomic's inner feelings anchor his speech. Their speech reveals that both are trying to adjust to fit what they feel is responsible for their behavior.

An integrated person might say, using variations of the above statements: "I sure feel turned on now . . . . I am bothered when I feel Bryan is too silent . . . . I am uneasy when I hear that dog yapping . . . . I want to laugh when I hear Cheryl laugh . . . . I feel uneasy when I see you use a fork that way . . . . I am frightened when I don't understand what you are going to do."

How an integrated person talks

Notice the way the integrated person talks about himself and his experience of the outer world. He links how he is experiencing an event with his perception of the event: *I am bothered* (a reaction to his inner experience) *when I feel* (integration of former inner experience) *Bryan is too silent* (a perception of the outer world). Talking with this dynamic flow of sensation building to an emotion, and *finding words* to fit the emotion, is the creative act of a person in touch with himself and others—in touch with his inner and outer worlds.

There seem to be other factors in the psychodynamics of Bryan's group that are important. Each person learned after several sessions to move back and forth between role and role-less behavior. This means that each person learned to use roles when he didn't quite know how to act or what to say. Each one felt comfortable sliding back into his personality until he found a way to express himself openly.

After a while the group members made allowances for this, and when one or the other drifted into the artificial behavior of his personality, they left him alone until that person could *find his own way* to express his feelings or respond rolelessly. This perhaps is one of the more important psychodynamics learned.

Roles aren't "bad." Personality isn't destructive. Bryan and the others learned to use the roles when they needed them – for protection, for shelter, to withdraw into until they felt strong enough to discard them. Jeanette mostly used her personality when interacting with Mac. Only some of the time could she relax and be "herself" when responding to Mac. But everyone came to accept this and not "punish" Jeanette for not being more at ease with Mac. Jeanette demonstrated some of the problems anomics have with verbals: She was strongly attracted to Les but, in contrast, was afraid of Mac; each verbal got a different response from Jeanette.

Roles have good uses, and the group (or any group) couldn't get along without them for long. But roles are artificial behavior, and are not the real person. The personal needs and deep relationships of each person in Bryan's group became apparent after each was able to discard his roles and reach the others as persons, not as personalities.

Similarity of intelligence is necessary

Another factor entered into the success of Bryan's group. All five persons had about the same range of intelligence. No one was much brighter or dumber than any of the others. Persons with low mental abilities or with very high ability usually are not able to interact well within small groups. There is a wide range of possible differences in intelligence, with extremes of persons having too much or too little. However, this has less importance as a factor in the dynamics of small groups than is generally supposed. (The final major consideration that aided Bryan's gestalt group was similarity of social-class background, which will be discussed later in this chapter.)

Thus far I have traced the paths of some of the specific psychodynamics of the group: how persons in Bryan's group were attracted to one another to interact within small diad or triad formations. For instance, there was strong sexual attraction between anomic Jeanette and verbal Les, a diad bond. Jeanette also was attracted to verbal Les because he seemed to be in touch with the outside world of how to do things, how to organize and carry out a plan, and how to learn new behavior. Les in turn was attracted to Jeanette, who seemed to be in touch with her inner world, something that Les missed in himself.

Opposites do attract

This is an example of the basic attraction between anomic and verbal persons, a strong sexual attraction based upon a sense of completing one's sexual self with another person who has what one lacks. Also, this anomic-verbal attraction extends further into how a person understands and copes with or is in touch with the outer world of doing things, manipulating objects, and so on. The anomic is drawn to the verbal because the verbal is in closer touch with the outside world. The verbal is drawn to the anomic because the anomic is in closer touch with the inner world of feelings and emotions.

As noted earlier, these kinds of bonds are strong and sudden, and frequently lead to a serious relationship. Les and Jeanette became lovers. This relationship probably had a rocky road with much conflict. Verbals and anomics do not understand each other's worlds, and have difficulty in establishing and maintaining deep communication.

Another diad bond developed between verbals Mac and Les. They understood one another better than either understood anomics Bryan, Jeanette, or Cheryl. In a like manner, anomics Bryan and Jeanette and Cheryl understood one another better than any of them understood Les or Mac. Anomics are in closer touch with their inner worlds and can get in deeper touch with others who also are anomic.

Anomics Bryan and Cheryl fell in love and had a good chance for an enduring relationship. They could share ideals and ways of doing things in their day-to-day life; neither would have been able to do this with verbal partners. Cheryl was an aggressive anomic and Bryan was a more passive anomic. It seemed a good fit, much better than Bryan and Jeanette, for instance, who were both nonaggressive anomics and very much out of touch with the outer world. Cheryl was a more integrated person than either. But, all became close friends.

The psychodynamics in Bryan's group may be clarified in the following:

A diad bond of *sexual attraction* formed between verbal Les and anomic Jeanette. This bond also included what could be called a complementary bond based on the melding of inner and outer world needs.

A diad bond of *love* formed between anomics Bryan and Cheryl. This had a sexual bond; there was sexual attraction between them, but this was not the most important nor most urgent satisfaction they found with one another.

A diad *friendship* bond formed between anomics Bryan, Jeanette, and Cheryl. This triad bond was anchored with the diad relationship between Bryan and Cheryl.

Note that these bonds were a mingling of different kinds of attractions each person had for another based upon his own inner needs. The persons in Bryan's group came together and found three very different kinds of relationships with one another but all fundamental in human behavior: *sex, love,* and *friendship.*

Social class and the group

Members of Bryan's group were helped in finding relationships with one another by all being from the same social class, which meant they had learned similar roles. I believe being male or female, and anomic or verbal, are the strongest determinants of how and why persons come together for deep relationships. But the roles they learn, and the personalities they create out of these roles, are the major factors that keep persons apart, and cause them to interact within their personalities rather than through their natural behavior. For instance, roles (that is, group ways of doing things) are transmitted primarily following the norms of a social class. Jeanette and Cheryl, for example, learned how to dress (choose and wear new clothes) according to the norms of their working-class families. In working-class families, the girls choose and wear what is fashionable, the fashions having already been set by tastes in the professional and upper classes.

A girl from the upper class, for instance, may wear clothes which not only are not fashionable, but which may be opposed to the current fashion. The roles for what to wear stem *from* what the more leisurely upper-class women are doing. They set fashion (roles of what to wear), and others tend to follow.

Major social-class divisions

There seem to be at least three major social-class divisions in which the roles transmitted to the old and young may differ widely. All of the persons in Bryan's group came from the same social-class background; all of their families were members of the "working class." Their fathers (and mothers, sometimes) worked at "jobs."

The other two divisions are the upper class (high society) and the professional class. Many behavioral scientists have more elaborate social-class divisions (some up to twelve distinct social classes), but for our purposes three divisions are adequate.

Les, Mac, and Bryan didn't dress alike, though Les and Mac dressed somewhat similarly. How they chose their clothes, the prices they paid, where they shopped and the clothes that were available there on the racks, all had some bearing on their choices and were similar. None of these three men had tailor-made clothes. Mac had handmade boots, and bought "mod" clothes from a men's wear shop. Les liked loud colors, and Bryan preferred bland colors, but all bought on the basis of how they were trained within their families and communities. However, Mac bought custom boots because they were *different,* and against the role he was taught while growing up.

All the persons in Bryan's group had similar roles for the table, or "eating" manners. For instance, they accepted the sharing of food from their plates. If someone left a portion of food, it was expected that another would eat it without qualms. But this is learned as a role: that it is all right for persons to eat from a common plate or bowl. In all their families it was accepted that someone would finish the food from someone else's plate if there were leftovers.

Bryan's group had no disagreements on the seemingly minor behaviors of eating, talking, dressing, going to the bathroom, touching, and so on. All of these human behaviors have roles specifically prescribed for them, roles of "what to do when." Each person made up a selection of the roles as his personality of social behavior. Some roles fit, some didn't; they differed with each person.

Class work roles differ

Mac, Les, and Bryan had fathers who taught them roles related to the working class. In this class, people work at skilled, semiskilled, or unskilled jobs, and are paid by the hour or occasionally on a yearly basis. Bryan's and Les' fathers worked and were paid so much per hour, and Mac's father got a yearly salary as a salesman. The working-class family has no other income unless another family member also works.

The professional social-class work roles are different: The fathers in this class usually work for salaries in some profession such as medicine, law, teaching, engineering, architecture, and so on. In the upper class, people have incomes not dependent upon a salary, but on investments or inherited wealth.

The work roles transmitted within these three social classes are vastly different. And this is true for virtually all the roles covering the whole range of human behavior, whether for male or female. Although there will be verbal or anomic personalities regardless of social class differences, the kinds of roles they adopt are prescribed by the social class. Therefore, the social behavior, the personalities of Mac, Les, Bryan, Jeanette, and Cheryl, were not so different as to create a barrier to getting along with one another in a gestalt group. The group members came together and interacted within their personality of roles before they could settle down and learn to relate to each other rolelessly, despite their natural tendencies which *transcend* social class, and which are common to human behavior everywhere.

Roles are sextyped

This brings us to an important consideration: All roles are sextyped, that is, there is specific behavior for a male or a female. This is true in every society. There is not just a way to do something, there are male or female ways.

For example, it is against the role norm in both the working class and professional class for females to belch or break wind in the presence of even their closest companions, whatever the relationship. But it is considered acceptable for the male to "relax" in close relationships and be "natural." Individuals may dislike these gaseous expressions, but the male does not violate a strong taboo when they happen. However it is unacceptable role behavior for the female.

In the upper class norm, the role is that expelling gas is a natural and highly private thing. Thus, an "accident" is not just ignored, it simply doesn't matter and is not worth noticing, for either sex. I cite this as an example because the strongest roles are the taboo roles surrounding male and female behavior in matters of sex, eating, and elimination.

Although all the persons in Bryan's group had similar role training, they had to struggle through their social personalities to reach one another as persons, not as personalities. As noted earlier, all roles are sextyped: role behavior is specifically defined as either male or female. There is a female way, for instance, to dress, eat, or make love. The roles for males are different in each case from roles for the female.

If this is true, then the sexual roles become the keystone to the development of personality in an individual. All of the persons in Bryan's group had similar roles taught them about their sexual behavior. Their families, churches, schools, and communities supported these sex roles. For example, Mac, Bryan, and Les were taught that it was all right for males to be interested in looking at the female body, including genitals.

But Cheryl and Jeanette were taught that girls not only should not look at male genitals, but that male sex organs are ugly. This is a specific role behavior defined by sex, and it is not the natural response of most females. In her sexual relations with Les, Jeanette had to cope with her response to the sight of Les' penis. She thought it was ugly because she was taught to think this way, regardless of how she might truly feel. When there is strong sexual attraction between male and female, such as that between Jeanette and Les, the natural response for both is a fascination with each other's sexual organs.

Also, both Jeanette and Cheryl were taught (roles) that girls waited until they were approached by males before they could establish a personal relationship; that the male had to initiate it. This is not the female role in the upper class, and the role is changing in the professional class so that the female may initiate a relationship when she chooses.

A cause of personality conflicts
within Bryan's group

It is my belief that the most difficult times that persons in Bryan's group had with one another came about because of their inability to discard their artificial roles of personality linked with their sexual behavior. This does not mean that all they wanted from each other was sex. It means that to find not just sex, but also love and friendship, they had to struggle with personalities that had at their foundation *a sexual character that was not real,* not representative of their inner needs.

Sex is but one component of human need, and if the personality is constructed around this, it seems difficult for a person to find a way to satisfy other needs that demand attention and want resolution. Bryan's group was fortunate. The members were able to find one another in ways that in-

cluded gratification of some sexual needs. But more importantly, friendship and love were discovered to some degree
by all. They were young persons and not as frozen into roles
as older persons usually are. Not all of the relationships in
Bryan's group would last, nor were all equally healthy for
each person.

Sex roles may control behavior

In most families, personalities of individuals are created
with *a basic network of sex roles* to control the individual's behavior *in all of his needs*. That this doesn't work well
for most persons seems obvious, what with the constant fascination they have with things sexual. The result is that sex
is easily and profitably linked to simple and natural acts
that have little to do with sexual needs, such as buying things
like cars, toothpaste, deodorant, insurance, and so on.

Let me note a few other items about Bryan's group before we move on. Mac and Les learned that their getting-
in-touch-with-themselves experiments differed from those
chosen by Jeanette, Cheryl, and Bryan. Mac and Les, being
verbals, and more out of touch with their inner world of feelings and emotions, found they had to practice finding out how
they felt about things or persons that they made contact
with — that it was a process of discovering what they felt
after making a contact with their food, or touching another
person. For instance, they had to learn to pick up a telephone,
think about how they felt about this telephone, and discover
that they *did have* a feeling about it which they once ignored
as being unimportant. Once they discovered they could feel
something about a simple telephone, they could find words to
describe their feelings.

The getting-in-touch process with Jeanette, Cheryl,
and Bryan, all anomics, all more out of touch with their
outer world, was different. These persons had to practice
making contact, for instance, with a telephone, then to find
words to fit how they feel about the telephone.

The verbal makes the contact but denies his feelings

about it. The anomic doesn't make the contact well. These are entirely different reactions. The verbal, remembering the telephone number, grips the instrument firmly, and dials briskly. But the anomic probably dislikes the telephone in the first place, so holds it loosely or awkwardly (or may drop it), dials incorrectly, and forgets the number.

The anomic does not make strong, clear contact with objects in his outer world. And this is what Bryan, Cheryl, and Jeanette had to concentrate on in their getting-in-touch experiments. For instance, they had to concentrate on making close contact with food, telephones, or what have you, to get the "feel" of the color, taste, firmness, or hardness, and then find words to describe this contact. Les and Mac had to learn that they felt something when they did make contact with objects or persons, to notice that there were feelings in the contact, and to find words to fit these feelings.

Recalling experiences in the group

Another area in which this group did well was in recall of pleasant and unpleasant memories. They found that they could resolve an *unpleasant memory* by continuing to recapture in minute detail the unpleasant experience by verbalizing it as if it were occurring in the present. They discovered that they could probe *pleasant experiences* through fantasy, thereby exploring their inner needs underneath their fantasy thoughts. This became one of the more exciting pastimes when the group met.

Jeanette, for example, discovered that her constant daydream of traveling in a jet across the ocean concealed a simple desire to get away from home and be on her own. She dropped this daydream and created one closer to her wishes: having her own apartment, what she would put in it, who she would invite there, and so on. She was happier and felt more satisfaction with this daydream than with the one she used before.

In the next chapter, we will examine artificial groups: what they are and how they compare with gestalt groups.

8

Artificial Groups

Ray and Irma Baxter had been married for eighteen years. They had worked hard and fought through many crises together to reach their common goal: the good life. Both came from working-class families where life was a bitter struggle to keep fed, clothed, and sheltered, and to get an education for the children.

They moved up through successive jobs and homes as Ray rose higher with his firm. Ray had about two years of college; Irma quit after one year when her first child was born. Ray's income as a general sales manager was beyond his fondest dreams, and enabled them to live in an upper middle-class suburban area. They had two cars, a boat, and a three-week vacation every year.

Their two children, Pam (sixteen) and Bruce (fourteen), studied seriously, got good grades, and planned to go on to college. Another child had died at birth. This pregnancy prompted an earlier wedding date than planned, and although the Baxters were disappointed over the infant's death, they were also relieved because they had wanted to delay having a family until they were financially better off. Pam and Bruce had been planned for.

The Baxters saved their money, planned ahead, and took

care of the important problems such medical checkups and insurance, but they were an artificial group almost from the start. (And they seem to be typical of most families.) Usually, the family group is the first natural gestalt group that arises from the social network of human relationships. A natural gestalt group is one in which the primary purpose is mutual care and concern. The other purposes, such as preparation for society, take a lower priority.

The Baxter family's major purpose was to create and train well-adjusted personalities. This purpose took precedent over love and care for each other as persons. The parents and children all cared for one another, but this was not their primary goal in being together.

An artificial group has primary goals independent of the individuals within the group, and standards which the individuals must measure up to, regardless of personal abilities or desires. For instance, Irma wanted to have a baby within the first year of marriage. But the couple had agreed to wait until they were financially better off before having children.

Ray started with his firm as a truck driver-salesman. He enjoyed the variety of contacts and persons he met during this period. But he took a cut in pay to accept a promotion that eventually led to an "inside" job with higher prestige. In both of these instances, Ray and Irma adjusted themselves to fit their ideas of what they should be. They adjusted to fit roles, rather than find roles to fit their natural needs.

Irma also wanted to continue college, but decided that a "good mother" (a role) stayed at home. She did not attempt to adopt roles in which she could have her children and also go to college, both of which fit her.

Problems under the surface

Each member of the Baxter family was adjusting to fit a conception of a good social personality. And on the surface, things seemed to go quite well. But several things were happening that they did not quite understand, and each family member was having greater and greater difficulty in his personal life. Each had to go outside the family group to find *natural gestalt groups* where he could relate to others outside his personality. (In artificial groups, the members relate to each other within their personality of prescribed roles.)

Ray had an old friend who was a truck driver-salesman for Ray's firm. They often went on hunting trips together. They were drinking buddies and would occasionally go on a binge. They would get drunk and weep and beat each other up like playful tigers, and were secretly proud of their occasional black eyes or split lips.

Ray also had a secret crush, a very sexual relationship with one of the office secretaries. They did nothing about this attraction, and had never even talked about it. But Ray was miserable when the secretary was not in the office. They did small, personal things for one another and developed an elaborate ritual of roles to avoid their true feelings, although they allowed touch contact now and then.

Irma had an old friend, a woman who was totally unacceptable to her husband or children. Irma tried to see her friend once every two or three months. They cared for one another, but the friend lived on the wrong side of the social tracks, and Irma felt she should not see too much of her.

Irma also had a male friend she preferred to see only occasionally. This friend worked for Ray's firm, too. Irma called him about every six months and they would have a sexual encounter, then wouldn't see each other until the next time. Irma had come to know it was time for one of these meetings when she started getting aroused by men on TV, in magazines, and even strangers on the street.

This affair bothered her, because she had regular sexual contact with Ray which she had learned to enjoy, and which she felt should satisfy her. Some of her strongest sexual aggressiveness toward other men came soon after she had had intercourse with Ray.

Pam was the better student of the two children. She didn't have any close friends outside the family. She bought a horse, took long rides, talked to her pony a lot, and virtually lived with it. Whenever Pam was troubled, she went to her pony and worked her problem out the best she could. She had intense sexual feelings that were solaced when she rode her pony or tended to its needs.

Bruce, the son, was in love with his cousin, a young girl who was on a lower rung of the social ladder, and a member of a family the Baxters no longer saw. He had mixed feelings about his cousin, sometimes confiding in her as a "sister," but often as not getting involved in hugging and kissing.

Natural gestalt groups sought outside the family

Bruce adopted another family in his neighborhood and secretly spent as much time with them as he could. This family lived down the block from him, and whenever he had problems he went to the woman and talked things over, and sometimes confided in her husband, too. They were a childless couple and delighted in having Bruce around. Bruce didn't have close male friends his age.

In every case, the members of the Baxter family group had to go outside the family to find natural gestalt groups in which they felt accepted and cared for as individuals. These relationships were "outside" personalities, and were essential if the individuals were to find gratification for their strong personal needs.

The primary purpose of a natural group is to provide the relationships to satisfy personal needs as they occur within group members. Ray developed roles of a good husband, father, and provider; and Irma as good mother, wife, and helpmate. The children became good students heading for college, obedient and kind to their parents. But Ray drank too much, Irma needed her occasional sexual encounter, Pam took pills, and Bruce smoked pot. And all had their only strong personal relationships outside their family.

This family was also struggling with the natural dynamics of small groups of persons living closely together. Early in the marriage there was an anchoring two-person (diad) bond of affection and interaction between Ray and Irma. When Pam was born, her parents accepted her as a third party in a triad (three-person) dynamic anchored by the diad bond of the parents. The parents could relate and find paths of affection to Pam, who, in return, got a "symmetrical" view of herself as both a male and female (Ray and Irma) viewed her.

But by the time Bruce was born, the natural gestalt family had changed its primary function to raising "well-adjusted personalities" instead of loving and caring for individual persons, which took a second-order priority.

Bonds within the family

The small group dynamics are at the same time obvious and deceptive. The parents, Ray and Irma, along with Pam, formed one of the strongest small groups, the triad. (My re search shows this is probably the strongest small group humans develop.) Then Bruce arrived to become a "fourth party." He was not included in the internal, personal bonds of affection enjoyed by Irma, Ray and Pam. The only personal bond Bruce had was a diad bond with his mother.

Now, if the family had retained its primary purpose of care and affection for individual members regardless of their personalities, Ray, Irma, and Pam probably would have found room for Bruce in the natural flow and change of small group processes, where the bonds are dynamic enough to permit members to move in and out as their needs shift and change. Actually, no one intended leaving Bruce out. But when the family adopted the goal of "raising the right kind of kids" as its primary purpose, what happened to individual family members subtly faded into the background.

By the time Bruce was born, Ray was moving up well in his firm. The parents made a point of being fair in the treatment of Pam and Bruce. Ray ignored the fact that he liked Pam better than Bruce, and Irma ignored the fact she liked Bruce better than Pam. (It could have been the other way around, not necessarily following the Freudian path. The kinds

of personalities each of the four developed, and their underlying individual traits, determined the small group bonds
more than sex characteristics.)

Personality tendencies affect relationships

Irma and Bruce tended to be more engrossed in their
inner world of feelings and emotions and to be under-integrated in their social behavior. They had anomic personalities. Ray and Pam tended to be engrossed more in their outer
world of objects and events, to be over-integrated in their
social behavior, and to have verbal personalities. *These
tendencies and subsequent personality development seem
to determine the bonds of attraction between persons more
than any other single characteristic.*

The personality differences are overcome when persons
interact with one another in families that are natural gestalt
groups. But when the emphasis in a family shifts, and it becomes an artificial group in which people interact with their
personalities of roles, personality differences then determine
how members are going to relate to one another.

The lines of relationship tend to follow personality dynamics, so that individuals do not relate to one another *as
persons,* but *as personalities:* as wife, husband, daughter,
son, etc. Those with the "best personalities" are the ones the
family believes should be supported the most. This drives
everyone to seek warm, affectionate gestalt groups outside
the family.

Let's return to the Baxters and their small group dynamics. Verbal Ray liked verbal Pam; anomic Irma liked
anomic Bruce. Ray was not a strong verbal personality; he
was not very successful in his outer world of things and
events. Ray did care for Irma; they had a diad bond between
them. But Ray cared more for verbal Pam; he understood her
better than he did Irma or Bruce.

So, Irma and Bruce cared for one another and understood
each other fairly well, but they couldn't really communicate.
Both of them deferred and let Ray and Pam make the major

family decisions. Pam and Bruce disliked one another, and didn't understand each other at all.

The family small group dynamic was fragmented into a series of two-person (diad) relationships, and a single, weak triad. Diads are dangerous; they do not seem to permit the rise and fall, the flow, of emerging needs of individuals.

Ray and Irma had the only sexual bond in the family that could be satisfied when need arose. Ray and Irma also had more diads: they had one with each other; Ray had one with Pam, and Irma had one with Bruce. Pam and Bruce had only one diad bond each: Bruce with Irma, and Pam with Ray. The children consequently had more difficulty living within their family than did the parents. In some families there are bonds between the children, too, but Pam and Bruce were not attracted to one another, so did not have a diad.

Now, the problems the individual members of the Baxter family had in creatively finding ways to satisfy their needs were compounded by the family emphasis on everyone having a well-adjusted personality. Problems are still present in a family that remains a natural gestalt group, but they generally find resolution as the persons grow and change, keeping their goal of personal care for one another as their primary purpose.

Family size is significant

A four-person family group has more difficulty than a three-person family or a five-person family. This is not a game of numbers, but rather a problem relating to the ease with which persons can relate and resolve conflicts among themselves. Some human needs, such as sex and intense love, are gratified only in a diad context. But even these gratifications are enhanced if found within a triad or five-person group that permits a flexible flow of response and reply without the one-to-one deadlock where unanimity must occur or the bond is weakened.

Diads are dangerous; if one person disagrees, the bond is broken. Triads seem the most effective, because there is room for disagreement without breaking up the bonds. Quads (four-person groups) tend to resolve into a triad plus one left out, or to break up into two diads. Next to the triad, the quin (five-person) group appears to have the best dynamic. The quin revolves around a diad-triad dynamic, two persons relating closely with one another but linked with a triad of three others involved more with each other. The triad joins the diad to form a well-balanced group.

Problems in groups larger than five

In groups of more than five, group members seem to react with their personalities rather than acting as individuals, whether they want to or not. For instance, in a six-person group, if it endures, a diad and a triad usually form, with the sixth person left out of the personal interaction.

In groups larger than five, members seem to have difficulty in communicating informally with one another, and end up talking to one another within their social personality of roles. Artificial responses and counterfeit encounters result. *Five persons seem to be the upper limit for group size in order for personal relationships between the individual group members to develop.* And, of course, anomics and verbals have different patterns within small groups. The verbal tends to enjoy groups larger than five because he interacts more with the outer world, using his personality of formal roles. The verbal shines in large groups; he basks in the glory of numbers.

The anomic tends to seek small groups, diads or triads, in which he can relate informally, person-to-person, outside his personality of roles. This dynamic is intensified if the group is artificial, where the members are interacting with one another within their roles of parents or children as in the Baxter family. The dynamic is less intense (though still present) when they can stand aside and relate to one another outside their personalities.

Success for the Baxters might come if they found a way to become a natural gestalt group, an opportunity that existed from the time the family first formed. It could mean that Ray should return to an outside job to get back in touch with himself—which he must do before he can get in touch with others.

It could mean that Irma should go back to college and find some outlet for creative needs not satisfied within her family. It may be that Pam and Bruce will have to grow older and leave the family and create natural gestalts on their own. The best course may be for Irma and Ray to help them do this as soon as possible.

Most family members do not care about one another as individuals. They don't fit one another, and, like the size of feet, this can't be changed. This is a tough lesson to learn.

Verbals Ray and Pam were caught up more in their outer world of events and objects. They communicated well with one another, and understood each other as did anomic Irma and Bruce, who were engrossed in their inner worlds of feelings and emotions. Ray and Irma loved one another, but they could have loved deeper if they were both verbals, or both anomics. Communication would have been so much better, as would the unspoken understandings. As it was, anomic Irma found her strongest sexual attraction with an anomic male, and Ray was strongly attracted to a "soft" verbal secretary. Both Ray and Irma turned to persons outside the family with whom they could get in touch more deeply. Pam and Bruce also turned elsewhere.

Ray's hunting friend was another verbal. Irma's girl friend was anomic like Irma. Ray, Irma, Pam, and Bruce all went outside the family group to find persons they could establish small gestalt groups with. If the family were not an artificial group, but had had as its first priority individual care for family members on a personal basis, then bonds of affection between Ray, Pam, Irma, and Bruce would have given each member some sense of loving and being loved in return.

Frequently, a weak bond pattern—in which there is no strong triad dynamic, but at least strong diads—is enough to hold a family in good stead. But in an "artificial" family, it is not enough. In many families, the parents have a strong diad and the children form diads or triads among themselves and they get along fairly well. But if there is a generation gap, family members get along only through role interaction of mother-father to son or daughter.

The Baxters were not an uncommon type of family; the members were struggling with personal tendencies and with small group processes they were only vaguely aware of, if at all. The anomics, Bruce and Irma, tended to blame themselves for their inadequacies, and the verbals, Pam and Ray, tended to blame others in the family. So it ended up that everyone blamed Irma and Bruce for the "failures" that occurred in answering the deep personal needs of each person. These conflicts were real, lasting, and inevitable as long as the family remained an artificial group.

The Smiths: A second example
of a family group

I'll describe briefly another family with a somewhat different small-group pattern, and with different personalities involved. Let's call them the Smiths. The two parents were verbals, but compatible, with the male a softer verbal than the female, who had a very strong verbal personality. They had two children, a verbal son and a younger anomic daughter. There was an anchoring diad bond of love and affection between the parents, but not much open expression of this. The parents had a good triad bond with their verbal son. The anomic daughter had always been "left out" of strong personal interactions in the family.

The parents related to one another as persons underneath their roles. The daughter observed this, and also that her brother was included in this bond, too. The girl was discontented with the incompleteness of her family relationships, so the family made room for her to maneuver, to find bonds in addition to those within her family.

The Smith family was a natural gestalt group, in which the primary goal was care and concern for each family member as a person, not just as a son or daughter, husband, wife, or parent. Whether they were being good sons or daughters, or good father-husbands or wife-mothers, was secondary to the greater concern of one for the other. There was no sense of sacrificing for each other in their family roles; no sense of doing things because it was someone's duty or obligation to behave in a certain way. The anomic daughter got along well with her paternal grandparents. She often spent her holidays and summers with them.

The Smiths came to this state of affairs easily over the years. They were more fortunate than most families, who struggle through life dissatisfied and disappointed with themselves and others, and never really know what happened to them. Most persons live out their lives in artificial groups. Natural groups arise from a person's network of social relationships. But, when persons in these "natural" groups relate to one another with their personalities, the nature of these natural groups changes to one of artificial encounters of role interaction.

Trudy and her problem with roles

Neighborhood groups can be natural groups. Young girls and boys come together because they live in the same block or district. Trudy, for example, was a girl of twelve who lived in a neighborhood for about a year. There were several girls near her age on her block, but she was unable to find a group who would accept her into their "clique." (Three neighborhood groups of girls already existed: a loose one of four girls, and two others with three each. None of these found Trudy acceptable.)

Trudy had an anomic personality and had not learned any strong roles which would allow her to be aggressive enough to penetrate one of these neighborhood groups. These were all artificial groups, since certain ways of dressing, talking, and acting socially were the primary requisites for entering the groups. Whether the new person was a good or bad human being was secondary.

Trudy's mother, Barbara, had a similar problem. Barbara also had an anomic personality and did not relate well in roles to the outer world of social behavior. She invited other mothers from time to time into a personal relationship "to have a cup of coffee," but after a year, she too had failed to penetrate a neighborhood group of her peers.

Trudy's father, Jim, was a verbal and thrived in the artificial groups at the office and in private social organizations such as the Elks. Jim had several roles with which to relate to others within his personality. He could be a good father, good employee, good friend, good Elk, good husband, and good citizen.

Trudy's relationship with her mother

Barbara and her daughter Trudy had each other and that was about it for them. They didn't like to move around, to change neighborhoods and cities, because they had so much trouble finding persons to have roleless relationships with. They both adopted fashionable ways of dressing long after the fashion faded, and then they did it badly, at least for them. They wore clothes that didn't fit their natural behavior. For instance, when hair fashions changed from bouffant to long, uncurled tresses, Barbara and Trudy struggled to have huge bouffant arrangements that outdid the original hair style, whereas less height would have fitted their small faces and figures better. They didn't understand how they got out of step because it was difficult for either of them to adjust themselves to fit new social roles, new group ways of doing things.

Nevertheless, Barbara, Jim, and Trudy were a close family, and had a strong triad relationship, anchored by the diad of affection between mother and daughter. It worked well but the females were discontented with their lives. Barbara didn't want any more children, and neither she nor Jim understood that she didn't want to disturb her bond with Trudy. This feeling was at a level of unawareness.

Barbara and Trudy had to find ways to contact persons with whom they could form natural groups. Trudy knew girls her age at school. She had to become aggressive and choose a few friends who fit her. A few were sufficient. Neither of these women could handle more than a few close relationships at any given time, but these few would brighten their lives. Barbara and Trudy were attracted superficially to verbal persons, because the verbals seemed so efficient. But verbals generally didn't relate well to them, if at all, and these attempts to establish friendships ended in wispy failure.

Anomics usually don't understand that it is not that verbals are so efficient (many are quite inefficient persons), but that the verbal relates to others *first* in a role, and later finds ways to reach out with his inner feelings or emotions. The process is just the reverse for anomics. The anomic is largely roleless, and has to relate first with his inner world of feelings or emotions before the relationship can move into the realm of roles and personality behavior.

Most persons, most of the time, come together in artificial groups. Interaction begins in an exchange of *roles,* that is, people respond to each other with their personalities, moving from artificial, formal ways of doing things *only* when the nature of the group changes to one of natural gestalt, wherein personal caring is possible.

An artificial group may become natural

Many artificial groups become natural groups after they have endured for some length of time. For example, Jim was on a committee in his firm that changed from an artificial to a natural group in less than a year. The committee was a work group that made out monthly reports on product costs. Jim and one other were verbals, but at the start there were four more, all anomics. The internal small-group dynamics didn't jell at first.

Jim and the other verbal formed a friendly diad, and the four anomics split into two diads. The group was at cross purposes even when deciding simple procedures. Three diads interacting couldn't reach common agreement. These were not open arguments; all used formal roles to avoid conflict.

This group of persons struggled for two months against the grain of their natural gestalt, and were only vaguely aware that they weren't "hitting it off." They were an artificial group because they had to use their roles of personality in order to be together.

One of the anomics dropped out when he moved out of town to another job. The three remaining anomics formed a triad and, along with the verbal diad, jelled as a five-person (quin) group. The anomics were in majority and were able, with the aid of the verbals' organizational ability, to tackle their formal goals.

Within six months, this group subtly changed from an artificial group to a natural group. They liked one another as persons, they discovered, and their meetings changed markedly. They abandoned the firm's conference room and began meeting late in the afternoon on Fridays at a nearby restaurant. They largely shed their formal roles, had a few drinks while working, and then had dinner together. This formed the basis for other groups. The anomics met socially first, and the verbals later, with their respective families. They got along well, and Jim's wife, Barbara, found a friend in the wife of one of the group's anomic males.

The evolution from artificial to natural gestalt – how this happens as persons come together in roles to interact with their personalities, then find ways of discarding their roles to relate to one another on the basis of personal needs – is a dramatic theme of human affairs.

But let's return to Trudy, the twelve-year-old daughter of Barbara and Jim. Her life was not at all unusual. She was anchored with a diad bond to her mother. She had trouble getting in touch with her peers, so had no close personal bonds with girls or boys in the community where she lived.

Trudy's problem in school

Anomic Trudy had an even bleaker life in school. There she was defined as a "slow learner," which was only part of the devastation she suffered. Most of her experiences at school were counterfeit, artificial, and unfelt by her. Her school (as are most) was organized around artificial groups.

Unfortunately, the major task of most teachers and the schools is the creation of personalities, the transmission of role behavior. This is almost without exception their primary assignment. The transmission of information that is the learning experience is a secondary assignment, in spite of all pretense to the contrary.

School teachers are mostly hired and retained on the basis of whether they can successfully transmit role behavior, that is, the proper ways of behaving with others in a school environment. A teacher may have creative talent in teaching information, but if he cannot organize his classroom, manage students, and teach them to fit themselves into the daily routines of standard achievement, the teacher does not fit in the system.

A teacher's job is to transmit role behavior

Probably the single most confusing task for a teacher to learn is that the transmission of how to behave in roles takes precedent over any learning that might occur. But this is the established goal of educational systems. And, as far as students are concerned, this makes their school experience artificial in the sense that they must adjust themselves to fit this goal, regardless of their own personal needs.

Trudy's classroom was an artificial group. She came in and sat with about thirty other persons. She was shy and seldom made friends even with students who sat at nearby desks. In a classroom of average composition, Trudy could expect to encounter more anomics than verbals. Anomics outnumber the verbals by three or four to one. This means that about seventy percent of the males and females in Trudy's class were similar to her in that they were engrossed in their inner world of feelings and emotions. They did not understand the outer world of facts, figures, objects, and events as well as the verbals.

Verbals shine where the primary assignment is learning roles. Standard achievement tests are based upon the accomplishments of the verbal personality, how well he succeeds in the variety of things he is taught about his outside world. The verbal is rewarded as the "good" student. He learns what he is told to learn, and in the ways (roles) that are accepted as proper. Although the verbal usually represents less than one-fourth of the class, the standards of measurement for all in the class are based upon the verbal's ability to understand events in his outside world as taught in the classroom.

Now, this presented some tremendous problems, not only for Trudy, but for the other anomics and for the school itself. And the verbals lost too, as will be seen. Verbals come to believe that it is not only desirable but natural to adjust to fit the outside world, not to adjust the outside world to fit them. Why shouldn't they come to believe in the "goodness" of this unhealthy process? Verbals receive the highest grades and the top awards for becoming "well-adjusted" personalities. And Trudy and other anomics receive a quite different kind of reward.

Dealing with "learning failures"

The schools have found ways of handling "learning failures" and have created a whole new breed of education specialists to deal with those who cannot absorb role behavior based upon classroom expectations. A number of categories have been created for these pupils: emotionally handicapped, educable handicapped, retarded, brain damaged, culturally deprived, emotionally deprived, and so on. And colleges train education specialists to deal with these children in the booming special education departments of the school districts.

Where the verbal is rewarded for his ability to interact within roles, the anomic is punished for his inability to adjust to role behavior. It is not just that the anomic is graded down, he is defined as abnormal. The anomic soon finds he is spending time with one or another of the fascinating range of specialists assigned to somehow correct his behavior. In Trudy's school, the latest trend was "behavior modification." This is a term that means the specialists use sophisticated techniques to get the pupil to adopt the "proper learning role behavior."

Trudy was not too much of a problem for her school; her offense was that she took days to learn things that a verbal or more aggressive anomic learned in an hour or two. Anomics range from those totally out of touch with the outer world, to the quiet anomic (like Trudy), to the aggressive anomic on the way to integration with his social and natural behavior. Verbals range from those totally out of touch with their inner feelings and emotions, to the hard verbal, to the soft verbal who approaches integration of his inner and outer worlds.

The totally out-of-touch verbal and all but the aggressive anomics are defined in special categories in schools. The strong verbal personality is too violent and frequently has to be removed from the school system. But the anomics are pliable, more "educable," and receive a lot of special attention because their number is so large.

Artificial groups in the classroom

Trudy's school groups were artificial even when the teacher broke the class down into small special-interest groups. Even then, the teacher selected who went into what group, which is against the grain of the natural gestalt dynamic. Trudy would have benefited greatly from being allowed to choose her own small learning group. If the teacher would have provided daily opportunity for Trudy to work with the persons she felt comfortable with, Trudy's learning ability would probably have been greatly enhanced. When this is done—when small learning groups are self-selected, not teacher-selected—specific changes usually occur. For one, more true learning takes place.

Classroom learning is a real problem for someone like Trudy. Conventional teaching is directed toward getting the pupil to adjust himself to the outside world of facts, or information, not toward adjusting the facts or information to fit the pupil's needs, his own unique way of understanding.

Verbals and anomics learn in different ways

As an anomic, Trudy had trouble adjusting herself to fit the outside world. Verbals tend to do this and become "better" pupils because this is the very dynamic of their relationship to the outer world. The verbal constantly attempts to adjust himself to fit the outside world regardless of his own personal inner experience of the situation. For instance, the verbal can learn "facts" about Indians regardless of how he feels about Indians. He accepts the fact that Indians exist independent of his own personal experience. But anomic Trudy had great difficulty with this; the only way she could learn much about Indians was to have an opportunity to envision *being an Indian herself,* relating whatever there was to be learned directly to her inner world. Trudy couldn't relate to information independent of herself. She couldn't adjust the way she reacted to fit some external idea of how things were, or should be. Trudy could learn something about Indians if, for example, she had a part in a play about Indians.

Trudy had to remake the information and find what part of it she understood in relation to herself. She could not learn information that she couldn't relate to in this way. The verbal can. He believes the world outside exists independently of himself, and he tries to adjust himself to fit it.

Most teaching experiences are directed toward verbal personalities who can pretend that the world outside exists independently of themselves. This means that fewer than one-fourth of the pupils in the so-called average classroom are able to learn adequately. Trudy was among the anomic majority of her class who had trouble adjusting to fit the conventional teaching-learning experience.

Pupils know what kind of learning suits them, and if given a chance and encouraged, will choose persons with whom they can learn best. The teacher can set the guidelines of what is to be learned, then allow the students to place themselves in small groups and choose the means and the pace for themselves. More learning will occur between pupils than any other way. These natural groups encourage self-confidence, friendship, and security in the classroom. It doesn't seem to make any difference as to overall class size, the dynamics of these small natural groups go on. However, the standard classroom learning situation blocks this dynamic and imposes an artificial group experience.

The dynamics of small groups

On the basis of my own research the following seem to be the natural dynamics of small groups everywhere: Diads are the least preferred small group size; triads are the most preferred small group size; quads are, after diads, the least preferred size; quins are, after triads, the most preferred. The same-sex triad, male or female, apparently is the best task-performing small group for specific learning such as math problems. The mixed-sex quin appears to be the most creative small group. *Members of groups larger than five persons tend to react in impersonal roles, and not to relate creatively to other persons or to assigned tasks.* Also, in groups larger than five, the persons tend to seek out diad encounters based upon roles rather than personal needs.

If the dynamics described are true of human gatherings everywhere, including the schoolroom, it is easy to understand how many persons live out their lives in artificial groups. In Trudy's case, it was unfortunate that she had artificial groups for her family and neighborhood relationships. It was even more unfortunate that she was confronted with artificial groups in school, and then defined as something less than normal.

Anomic Trudy was person oriented, not object oriented. She was affective, subjective, inner-directed; not cognitive, objective, outer-directed. She probably would have had a high IQ, near 130 perhaps, if there were tests to measure her brand of ability. However, she was tested against verbals, who represent less than twenty-five percent of all students, and she came out with a less-than-average score.

A major problem for Trudy was revealed in this artificial group experience in school. Although she might have found reasons for her failure to have close personal relationships with her family or neighborhood friends (such as, it was no one's fault the family moved around so much), the impact of the school was inescapable. In school she was defined by her society as less valuable than the more desirable verbals. This seemed to Trudy to be an impersonal judgment, beyond her power to correct, beyond her ability to understand. Even if she worked out close personal relationships with others, she was on the defensive, acting through fear and guilt, rather than according to her current needs, whatever they were.

Sensitivity groups and the Baxters

I have described thus far how persons in families, in neighborhoods, at work, and at school are confronted with mostly artificial groups, wherein they fail to find close human bonds with one another to answer their needs for care and affection as individuals. Let me return now to Ray and Irma Baxter and describe their experiences with "sensitivity" groups.

When the group phenomena of marathon weekends, encounter groups, sensitivity groups, and so on first began to spread in the 1960s, Ray and Irma Baxter jumped at the chance to find a "meaningful emotional experience." Most of their married life together had been a struggle to get close to each other, but as noted in earlier paragraphs, their family was an artificial group concentrating on everyone having a "well-adjusted personality," rather than on individual concern and care for family members. They found themselves lonely and out of touch with each other as they interacted within their roles as husband and wife, and mother and father, instead of as two persons with real needs for a close human bond.

For several months they sampled different kinds of pop groups and inevitably ended up having counterfeit experiences. Of the many artificial groups the Baxters already had at home or work, these "sensitivity groups" became perhaps the most artificial of all. The Baxters spent a lot of time and money together in couples' groups, or separately, trying to find "magic moments" of emotional release or renewal.

Encounter groups are unsuccessful for several reasons

The cards are stacked against persons finding close human bonds in these groups, and in many cases the experience adds to the problems the person has in the first place. This is true for several reasons, some of which appear obvious. First, in a game group or a growth group, or in a group with a combination of these two approaches, usually (if not always) group members are required to interact with a "leader" or someone with such a title. Someone is in charge giving directions, interpretations, and analyses of what's going on. Unless the "leader" gets out of the way and abandons his role as leader, group members seldom can respond to one another in whatever healthy dynamic there might be between and among them. If some "expert" is in charge of the group, this situation in itself blocks the emergence of a healthy dynamic within the group. (This is a hard lesson to learn, and to change this technique means changing the financial and emotional rewards enjoyed by group leaders.)

Many of the self-styled group leaders are charismatic individuals who delight in being the center of attention in addition to getting paid for their performance. Some of the worst leaders are psychologists or psychiatrists (who should know better). But group sensitivity sessions are very much a part of the money tree now, and it is difficult for persons in these professions not to respond to this trend although they may be untrained, unknowledgeable, and without skill in small group processes.

A second defect creates just as much difficulty, even if

the group leader is highly skilled: Persons in these groups usually do not know one another before they meet and do not see each other outside the group experience. This in itself blocks the development and emergence of close human bonds.

Unless the relationships formed within the group are buttressed by other day-to-day contacts with one another, what happens during the group meetings becomes progressively more artificial. The weak bonds that might grow into friendship or love are never strengthened. It is much like going to a movie or a football game: You pay your money, have your "experience," then go home and wait 'til next time, until the next movie or game. This *fragments* rather than encourages enduring human responses.

Successful group experiences come when leadership emerges from members of the group and is shared as the group continues. And successful groups emerge when the group members have come to know one another through some natural grouping in their everyday lives. The professional group leader can help groups get started, but if the leader doesn't stand aside and get out of the way of the dynamics between the group members, the group fails.

A third obstacle

There is a third serious obstacle blocking the healthy dynamics in the typical "sensitivity" group. Most planned encounter experiences have eight, ten, twelve, or more persons involved in the sessions. One of the more significant findings in my research is that when persons attempt to respond to one another, the size of the group determines whether or not the persons can relate informally to each other. The most consistent evidence shows that when there are more than five present. formal role behavior dominates their responses.

When persons relate to one another in roles, they are not acting in concert with their inner responses or needs. In other words, no real communication or deep understanding of one another is possible if more than five persons are involved in the dynamic. In groups larger than five, the persons involved tend to break down into diad or triad groups. It seems that the five-person quin, containing a diad and a triad, is the upper limit in size if informal small-group processes are to survive.

Any one of these circumstances — *structured groups* with specific things to do, *led by a "leader"* with *more than five persons* involved — is sufficient to block the emergence of enduring human bonds. And as noted many times, most groups, most of the time, contain all three of these barriers to healthy group processes.

The results of the Baxter's group experiences

The Baxters, especially Ray, at first enjoyed their group weekends and other sessions. He and Irma developed their own roles as "good group members" and responded to others with this added "personality." They followed the crowd to various popular leaders of the moment. Anomic Irma found she was talking less and less with Ray. About the only conversations they had during their "group" period were about what had gone on in the most recent group session. Ray and Irma would "open up" to strangers and "tell all," and were led to believe that this would give them emotional growth. It took several months for them to realize that they hadn't developed a single enduring bond with anyone from the many groups they had joined.

Anomic Irma stopped going first and blamed herself for not being able to get much out of her sensitivity sessions. Verbal Ray liked to meet new persons and talk about himself, so he continued sampling new groups from time to time; but even he tired of meeting the same or similar persons making the circuit with one leader, then another. He finally got all "talked out" and bored with himself, and quit.

The Baxter experience is the most common and typical outcome for most persons involved in the group movement. It was harmless for the most part in their case. Some persons derive brief joy or benefits, while others may become severely disorganized emotionally from the experience. But true benefit or serious harm occurs much less frequently than the sterile middleground as experienced by the Baxters. They were seeking enduring personal growth and this cannot be found within artificial groups interacting with one another in stereotyped roles.

9

Anomics and Sex, Friendship, and Love

Ron and Karen had been married for thirteen years, and had two boys. Ron was thirty-five and Karen thirty-three. Ron had been a school teacher for fourteen years, while Karen had never held a job. She married Ron immediately after graduating from high school, and since then had been busy being a housewife and mother.

Ron liked his work and planned to make it his lifelong occupation. Karen liked being a mother and wife, and had no desire to be anything else. But both were discontented with themselves and each other, and had been most of their marriage. Ron liked to read and discuss educational books and magazines. Karen didn't like to read. She seldom even read the newspaper. She wasn't interested in politics or national affairs, and trusted that "things usually work out for the best." Neither one did things the other cared for. Nor could they do things together. For instance, when they went on a trip, it ended up a minor disaster. In no time at all, they got bored with each other, packed up their clothes, and rushed back home to end the pain.

Ron became furious with Karen because she wouldn't read, or "get out of her cave" to find out what was going on in his world. Both were deeply puzzled over their relationship. As you are probably aware, Karen had an anomic personality, and Ron was a verbal. They had a strong sexual attraction for one another and enjoyed sex, but they had a sense of incompleteness in their sexuality, and in the marriage itself.

Ron worried because he was constantly attracted to other women. At times he thought about getting a divorce. He was tempted to date a female teacher he worked with. She had an anomic personality, and Ron felt sexually drawn to her, and she to him.

Karen was aware that Ron had "a roving eye." This troubled her, and she wondered about herself, too. She had two or three casual friends, males, whom she saw in her daily routine and who interested her more than she cared to admit. She liked to talk to the butcher at the meat market; she thought he was attractive, quiet, modest, and easy to know. She also liked their insurance agent, too much she thought, and she often had daydreams about a current movie star, whose films she had seen several times. All of the men she was drawn to were anomics, like herself. There was no strong sexual component in her attraction to these friends; rather there was a feeling of closeness, with sexual feeling vaguely in the background. Karen was afraid Ron would leave her someday, and Ron worried because he often thought about leaving, too.

Ron and Karen's problem is not unusual. It stems from one of the most common human errors when choosing a marriage partner: They chose each other for the wrong reason. Verbal Ron and anomic Karen were strongly attracted to each other sexually when they first met. And they continued to have this attraction. (Verbals are more sexually attracted to anomics than they are to other verbals. The same seems to be true of the anomic.) Anomic Karen was more sexually attracted to verbal Ron than to any of her casual male acquaintances.

Along with this strong sexual attraction between verbals and anomics, there was a sense of completing the missing parts, a kind of filling in where each felt there was a lack. For instance, because anomic Karen was absorbed in her world of feelings and emotions, and did not make firm contact with her outer world of objects or events, she could not clean a house well, nor did she know how to handle cooking utensils such as pots and pans, measuring spoons, or can openers. She wasn't able to keep an accurate budget or checkbook, and so on.

Karen first had to relate the things of the outer world to herself before they had any meaning for her. She was not only strongly attracted sexually to Ron, she also relied on his knowledge of the world. He knew how to do things, how to cope with the outer world of cleaning houses, making appointments, doing necessary mathematics, putting things together, and meeting new people. Karen did not know how to do these things competently and Ron did, so she respected and admired him for his ability. Karen felt she needed someone like Ron, who could cope with the outer world where she was so awkward.

Ron's attraction to Karen

Ron was absorbed in his outer world, but was out of touch with his feelings and emotions. He was attracted to Karen because she seemed so much more in touch with her inner world than he was with his own. He respected and admired her for being able to "feel things through." He saw this as a weakness, however, and as something women could do naturally, and men couldn't.

Ron felt that most women were similar to Karen: sensitive, quiet, modest, and socially withdrawn. Karen sort of believed this, too. (These myths are difficult to penetrate and destroy.) Ron and Karen both were reared to believe that good marriages must be founded on a strong sexual attraction plus respect and admiration for one another, and that this indubitably led to successful marriage.

Not only did Ron and Karen have trouble as marriage partners, they weren't even good friends. They couldn't talk with one another. They did not share the same worlds. Ron was absorbed in the outer world and Karen was absorbed in her inner world. Things had to "go right" in his job, for instance, before Ron felt right about himself. And Karen had to have a secure sense of her inner feelings before she was comfortable in the world of people or events. This was a fundamental difference between the two.

Karen explained things by how the events fit her inner responses (her feelings and emotions). Ron explained things by measuring how well they fit what he understood about the outer world and its operations.

Karen and Ron were good sexual partners. But verbals and anomics usually learn to distrust one another and frequently openly dislike or hate each other. Unable to find close friendship with one another, they seldom build a love relationship. Ron tended to be sadistic, to enjoy causing pain. He felt sexually excited when he was punching, pushing, biting, or chewing on Karen. She tended to be masochistic, to enjoy being in pain. She felt sexually excited when Ron did these things to her. Although she disliked violence, she was sexually excited when she was hurt a little bit, or even a lot. Pain sexually excited her. When Ron unintentionally got too rough she objected, but he learned that her objections masked a strong sexual emotional response that she herself avoided recognizing. So, although Ron and Karen were sexually attracted and had a certain amount of respect for the orientation each possessed in their respective worlds, it was not enough.

The verbal dominates the anomic

The verbal-anomic relationship also is dependent upon dominance of the anomic by the verbal. There is little sharing or equality. Ron wanted to dominate Karen and she invited this domination. It was a cruel circle. There was little sense of cooperation between them, and no deep understanding or communication. These are imperative between friends, and persons in love. Ron and Karen simply did not understand one another. There was a barrier between them that they couldn't tear down. They could not reach each other's respective worlds.

What should they do to escape their dilemma? It does no good to say that they should have enjoyed sexual relations during their romance, and then married other persons. Sometimes a couple trapped in a marriage of this nature, after several years of being at a "stuck point," divorce and go their separate ways. Sometimes, too, after separation, they return to each other to satisfy their strong sexual attraction.

Some possible solutions

Ron made several wrong moves. He did not have sex as often with Karen as he really wanted, because he thought that he would get bored with her, and wouldn't find her sexually attractive. If he wanted his marriage to work, he was going to have to find one or two women with whom he could be close friends—verbals like himself who could share his outer world orientation, and who were not too concerned about their feelings or emotions. He would enjoy sex with a verbal woman; but also he would enjoy a broader range of closeness and understanding, and sex would not play a too significant a part in the relationship. Verbal Ron would not find a verbal woman as sexually attractive as anomic Karen.

For her part, Karen could develop closer relationships with anomic males—a direction in which she already had started. She could find a sense of closeness, of friendship and caring with an anomic male, that she didn't have with Ron. Karen also could experience joy in a sexual relationship with an anomic male, but here again, she enjoyed Ron more than she would an anomic male. This may appear a somewhat perverse reversal of what marriage should be.

Sex is a pressing need that must be responded to, but sexual satisfaction could not begin to fill the needs both Ron and Karen had for closeness, understanding, a sharing of views, deep personal security, shelter, warmth, affection, and a strong sense of identity with one another. If the idea of divorce was too threatening for them, perhaps they could find their way toward creating new relationships with other persons that fit their respective needs. If they could have learned to tolerate the incompleteness they felt with one another, and to allow each other to find ways to fulfill needs, they might have held the marriage together.

A limited relationship

But this was a somewhat artificial adjustment. They didn't love one another; they weren't even good friends. There was a pattern of dominance (by Ron) and submission (by Karen) in their personalities of roles. They could enjoy their sexual compatibility and the mutual regard each had for the other's abilities. This kind of relationship always seems to have jealousy as a third partner. Ron and Karen, sensing an incompleteness, and aware of their strong sexual attraction, were each plagued with constant jealousy and fear that the other person was seeking another sexual partner. This would have been the least of their worries if they truly understood one another.

Ron tended to "get right at" sex, briskly, turning in a "good lasting performance." This was exciting for Karen, but when he was done, he got up, bustled about feeling good and strong, and busied himself with other things. Karen would have liked Ron to stay with her to soak in close contact and talk and caresses, leisurely winding-down after their sexual experience. If they had shared inner or outer worlds (if they were both either anomic or verbal), they would have been more likely to agree on how to bring their sexual activities to a satisfying close. The role patterns of verbals and anomics seem to doom closeness.

Anomics like Karen tend to adopt childlike dependency roles. Ron called her his "baby." She liked being called this, and liked being treated as a person who needed help in the outer world. Verbals such as Ron tend to adopt adult authority roles in which they dominate other persons. Karen called Ron "daddy" and he liked this.

The important point here was for Karen and Ron to quit worrying about their sexuality and drop their jealousy. Sex was their basic attraction and strongest support. If they wished to stay together, they should have set about creating new relationships with other persons that would satisfy their respective personal needs. However, it is sometimes very difficult to break off a failed role relationship, such as Karen and Ron had, in marriage.

If they wanted to patch up their shaky marriage, they had to gratify one another's deeper needs. Ron already had several male friends who were verbals like himself. But he needed to develop some relationships with verbal women. The difficulties of such relationships are obvious, however. To be involved in a love relationship while continuing his marriage to Karen, though possible, would not have been practical.

Much the same was true for Karen. She already had created some anomic male relationships which she could have expanded. She also needed to build new bonds with some anomic females. Karen said she didn't like women. But, in reality, she needed to have at least one, if not two, women friends to feel close to.

The marriage I describe above is not unusual. Persons get married all the time for the wrong reasons; the most common seems to be that they misinterpret sexual attraction for love.

A second example: Roger and Eve

Let me describe another marriage. Roger and Evelyn (Eve) had been married ten years. Roger was a "soft" verbal, a fairly well-integrated person, but still more in touch with the outer world of persons, things, and events than with the feelings and emotions of his inner life. Roger was growing closer to balanced integration the older he got (he was forty at the time of this account). For most of her life, Eve was a nonaggressive anomic, but as she grew older (she was thirty-six) she moved closer to being an integrated person too, becoming an aggressive anomic and getting in closer touch with her outer world of persons and events.

Roger was a journalist. And Eve was a secretary until she married. This was a second marriage for Roger, and Eve's first. She was an involuntary career girl, and would have married sooner if she could have been free of family burdens that had trapped her for years.

When Roger and Eve met they experienced the anomic-verbal sexual attraction but in different degrees. Roger's sexual feeling for Eve was stronger than her's for him, although she found him attractive. Her strongest attraction to Roger was friendship combined with the typical anomic's admiration of the verbal's ability to cope with the outer world of things and persons. Her strongest first impression of Roger was that she "trusted him" and could "relax" when she was with him.

Friendship was possible

Roger, along with his sexual feeling for Eve, was attracted to her because she was in touch with her inner feelings and emotions. Roger sensed a closeness, an immediate feeling that they could be close friends. They both saw more in the relationship than just a casual encounter. A strong sense of friendship was possible here because Roger was not a "hard" verbal and Eve was not a weak anomic. (Restated, Roger was a "soft" verbal and Eve an aggressive anomic.) This resulted in quite a successful mixture of sex, love, and friendship.

Roger did not plan to remarry. He had married a strong verbal woman the first time, and realized too late that although there were similarities, she was too verbal for him, too out of touch with her inner world of feelings and emotions, too absorbed in the outer world of material things. However, Roger felt deeply about Eve the first time they met and changed his plans easily about remarriage.

On Eve's part, when she met Roger, she was already involved in a sexual relationship with a married man, a verbal.

When she met Roger, she quickly dropped this affair in favor of one that held promise of marriage and a more lasting relationship. She had always been attracted sexually to verbal males, and to *anomic males or females for friends*.

Roger had one or two anomic male friends, but most were verbals. He was attracted sexually to anomic women, but since his thirties, sex was less important to him as the *basis* for a relationship. His sexual feelings for Eve, along with his feelings of friendship, were a pleasant surprise. And Eve was delighted, too. She had found someone who seemed to fit her needs in her inner and outer worlds in a combination she hadn't found available before. Thus, each had good reasons for getting married. There was a strong bond of friendship between the couple, along with sexual attraction, though in different degrees.

The friendship bonds between Roger and Eve grew stronger over the years and theirs became a love relationship. It was neither a quick nor easy transition because there were still basic differences. Roger, as a verbal, tended to relate better to the outer world of persons and events, and Eve tended to relate better to her inner world of feelings and emotional responses.

Uneasiness in their sexual relationship

There was some uneasiness and misunderstanding about their sexual relationship. For a long time, Eve didn't think Roger was very sensual since he didn't seem to want much sex; and when he did, the encounter was over within a few minutes. Many times when Eve wanted sex, she didn't say so because she felt that Roger should be the one to initiate sexual activity. She wondered if he really loved her. Roger was uncertain, too. Sometimes he seriously doubted that Eve loved him. He had been intimate with other women, and Eve didn't seem to be as sexually attracted to him as they had been.

There was another problem which vexed them. Eve welcomed oral sex provided she was the recipient; however, she found reciprocating in kind distasteful. Oral sex from Eve was not as exciting for him as was his oral sex with Eve, or their "normal" intercourse. Eve's apparent attitude of not enjoying him in the same way as he did her, that is, her avoidance of oral sex, caused him to wonder. In sexual activities with other women, he had experienced a variety of oral sexual behavior.

Roger didn't expect Eve to perform as these other women had, but he wondered why she had never seemed as fascinated with him sexually as he was with her. He understood that he was pleasant sexually for Eve, but he saw this as a kind of friendly sex, a sex-between-friends sort of relationship, not urgent, or pressing, or filled with intense passion. Though she was willing to do anything he asked, in more than ten years of marriage, she had never revealed any strong sexual attraction, on impulse, for Roger that he could see. While in Eve's view, Roger didn't seem to want very much to be touched, to be close and to hug and kiss.

The "stuck point" surfaces

Finally, the hidden "stuck point" between them surfaced, and was a surprise to both. Neither was aware of the other's doubts and emotions surrounding what seemed to be a good marriage relationship. One night, while they were discussing what specifically Eve liked to do during sex, Roger realized Eve was integrating a sexual experience with another lover ten years previously. On recalling the experience, she was flushed with excitement in a way Roger had never seen before. This stunned him because he had always thought he was everything sexual to her. The thought that some other man had satisfied her more than he could was a blow to Roger. But it fit with his other doubts about how much he really attracted her sexually.

Roger also realized that he was occasionally bored with Eve's world, and she with his. Eve protested his reactions to her sexual integration of a past experience, insisting her desire was for him and not for a past lover. Subsequently they spent many hours discussing, thinking, and working through their experiences with one another, and returned to Roger's disenchantment with himself. Eve finally wanted to drop the issue and get things back on their prior basis. And Roger wanted this too.

Eve and Roger were in love, and had a good chance of understanding each other's sexual feelings. That they got bored with one another's worlds now and then seemed normal, for they were absorbed in different worlds; Eve in her inner world, and Roger in the outer world. This condition did not make them uneasy nor cause either one to expect the other to change. They were not *that* bored with one another. Although Eve tended to be anomic and Roger verbal, neither was too far out of touch with their inner self to prevent contact with another's needs.

Sex was secondary to love

Roger didn't usually require a lot of sex; his interest in sex was not a barometer of his love for Eve. He did find his wife sexually attractive, and she fulfilled most of his sexual needs. He didn't seek extramarital contacts. Though Eve was more sexually attracted to stronger verbal males, she also found Roger pleasant and would not jeopardize her marriage. Their sexual relationship was secondary to their deeper love relationship. For somewhat different reasons, their sexual needs matched, that is, they fitted in a complementary way.

Eve was ready to adjust herself to be a perfect sexual partner in whatever way Roger wished. But he didn't want her to do anything that didn't originate in her own feelings, and Eve had to be careful not to play a role of "sexy woman." They faced the possibility of a counterfeit experience if this occurred. They had no false experiences in their other relationships with each other.

It is not serious that Roger and Eve didn't understand each other's sexuality as well as they did all the other ways they came together. But his seemed a small "imperfection," one that could be corrected in time. Sexual understanding is not necessary for a deep relationship; this may be one of the most difficult things to understand. Every human relationship has some area of incompleteness. Too many relationships stagger under the burden of the individuals trying to comprehend every facet of their mutual attraction or deficiency with each other.

Roger and Eve let the gestalt of their sexuality emerge on its own. There was love there and that was the stronger gestalt; it would shape the rest of their relationship to fit their needs if they allowed it to happen. If they didn't, they would needlessly hinder their lives together. Since Eve's sexual requirement was moderate, she felt secure if she felt loved and needed. Roger's unease with his own sexuality was the focus of the problem in the first place.

Roger was much less interested in sex than he had been in his younger days. He hadn't the drive he once had years before, and he wondered if his virility was diminishing. This problem couldn't be separated from Eve, but it was not her problem, and that was difficult for Roger to accept. He also had to accept Eve as she was, including the fact that she was attracted sexually to stronger verbal personalities than Roger, but that attraction was not the most important thing to her. Roger had to accept that she far preferred to have her marriage and the love and friendship she found there, and was not seeking other sexual companions.

What Eve wanted to learn

Once, in talking with Eve about herself, I asked her to write down what she most wanted to learn: She wrote:

1. What the process of learning is so I can learn anything I set out to learn.
2. How to have a group of people (more than two or three) who care for me.
3. How to be in touch with myself and my surroundings so I can enjoy everything more.
4. How to understand people so I can cope with anyone who comes along.

5. How to be in touch so that I can cut through any mystery that surrounds anything and get to the core of it.
6. How to understand everything about me.
7. How to understand people quickly so I can cast off the uninteresting ones.

This is a long list with items that overlap and repeat. It revealed her basic concerns as an anomic personality. She was in close touch with her inner world of feelings and emotions but out of touch with how to cope with the outer world of persons and events. Her central concern was to know how to choose persons who fit her. This seems to be a major problem with most persons.

People find it difficult to know how to judge whether or not someone else will fit them and fulfill their needs for sex, love, or friendship. There are two major preconditions: A person must be able to identify whether he himself is anomic or verbal and then whether others are anomic or verbal. These are very different. A person usually has to understand what he is first before he can understand what others are, and recognize in them either a similarity or dissimilarity.

How to recognize anomics

In the examples above, both Eve and Karen were anomics with seemingly different personalities, but there were basic similarities. In general, they did not learn how to do things easily. They took longer than verbals to learn to ride a bicycle, type, play tennis, drive a car, keep a budget or checkbook, and so on.

Anomics have trouble learning how to coordinate with activities in the outside world. They do not make good contact with objects. They drop things, don't clean surfaces well, don't hammer hard enough with a hammer, don't scrub hard enough.

Anomics Eve and Karen learned to ride bicycles, clean their homes, cook, and so on only after considerable practice and frustration. They had to work hard over a long period of time to develop these learned skills. Anomics Eve and Karen could always spot another anomic by the way the person tried to organize the outside world. It was a dead giveaway. Anomics may come to learn a complex skill, but they pay a heavier price than verbals in time spent. Eve and Karen had poor memories. They both had bulletin boards in their homes, and made lists before they went to a store.

Anomics do not have a good sense of passage of time. Eve and Karen missed appointments, or were too early or too late. They did not organize their time before going somewhere and did not know how long it took to get ready to go. Both would get dressed to go out, make a list of things to do, and places to go, then find they hadn't allowed enough time to accomplish the tasks they set.

Anomics fear violence. Eve and Karen could not bear the sight of blood. They did not like games of violence. War and men at war were mysteries. The killing or hurting of persons or animals was painful for them to observe or think about.

Eve and Karen both tended to respond too soon to their feelings, before they allowed an emotional reaction to set in. If a restaurant were dirty, they wouldn't eat the food, no matter how good it was, not because they believed that a restaurant must be clean to serve good food, but because they lost their appetites. A verbal might decide that every dirty cafe has dirty food, and then not eat there for that reason, regardless of his appetite.

Sexual attraction is often mistaken for love

Eve and Karen tended to believe they were in love when they experienced a strong sexual attraction, without waiting until their feelings about the person were clear. Anomics may say they have been in love several times, and mean it. Typically, they feel they have been in love far more frequently than do verbals. Anomics have a history of broken love affairs. It is very important for them to feel they are in love with someone at any given time, even if down deep they know it isn't true love.

Anomics tend to drift into occupations in which they can relate personally to the work itself or to persons on the job. Eve liked those jobs where she could relate personally to her boss or to her coworkers. She didn't like typewriters, bookkeeping, filing, or most of the office routines. She was happy doing these things only if she felt she was doing them for someone she cared for and who cared for her as a person. Eve would never join a secretarial association, for instance, because she didn't feel a sense of belonging to a general category of "secretaries" as an occupation or profession. Both Eve and Karen would do well working in a small shop or business where the contact between customer and employee would be on a personal basis. Anomics need personal contacts whether casual or formal.

Karen's and Eve's roles

There are, however, differences between Karen and Eve. Karen was more anomic than Eve, more out of touch with her outer world. Karen had only one role that fit her, that of being a mother. Her roles as Ron's wife, sexual partner, and friend were weak and fragmented because of her underlying feelings of insecurity.

Karen was typical of many anomics: she could talk fairly well about herself and things related to her "mother" role, but she was silent or only a little vocal when she was not acting within this role. She could talk easily and volubly about her children and their relationship, and what they do or plan together. She talked easily with Ron about these things. But Karen could not express herself well outside this "mother" role, so she and Ron had difficulty talking to each other.

On the other hand, Eve was an aggressive anomic who found several roles that fit her. She had a "wife" role, a friend role, and a "sexual partner" role with Roger. All of these fit her and she was comfortable in them and could talk easily within them.

Eve usually recognized other anomics, male or female,

and could assume a "friendship" role with them, and talk quite easily about whatever business there was at hand. But Eve had no roles for the verbal persons she met, except perhaps her sexual role, and this, of course, was inadequate for routine social contacts. She sometimes admired verbal persons but lacked roles necessary to interact with them. She did not like verbal women at all and avoided them.

Anomics and sex

A major point concerning anomics and sex is that anomics prefer having things done to them, rather than doing things to other persons. Attitudes about solitary sex are examples of this tendency. Karen never masturbated. She thought that manipulation of body parts was something boys did *to* girls, or to themselves. After several years of marriage this was still her attitude.

Eve, however, masturbated regularly before she was married, worried about it, and struggled with guilt feelings. She wouldn't use her hand to stimulate herself, but always an object because she had been taught that she shouldn't touch herself "down there," that it was dirty and sinful. Neither Karen nor Eve liked to manually stimulate their husbands, but both women very much enjoyed having these things done *to* them.

The sexual patterns of Karen and Eve illustrate why the anomic is so strongly attracted sexually to verbals rather than to other anomics. Verbals like to do what anomics want done. It seems to be a fundamental attraction.

Karen was not an aggressive anomic and was somewhat socially isolated. She did not seek sexual contact or even friendships outside her marriage. Eve, an aggressive anomic, had a different story. Eve learned how to recognize verbal males. She always had been aware that certain kinds of males stimulated her more than others, but only in later years did she come to understand what happened in this attraction.

Roger was not a strong verbal; he was much less aggressive in his handling of the outer world than a more verbal male. Eve was strongly attracted to the aggressive, seemingly powerful male who dealt with himself and his environment with great ease and skill.

When Eve came into a room of strangers, she knew how to spot the upper and upper-middle class verbal males. To her, these males seemed to be in command of themselves. They walked and stood in a certain "masculine" way. They talked with strangers easily, and they seemed to do things for people around them, such as lighting cigarettes, getting drinks, and helping organize food serving.

The strong verbal male handled things well, Eve believed, and had good manners, knew what to say, and filled in conversational gaps. Eve said that these men seemed to be clean, "smooth," and capable of coping with the world to satisfy their needs. Eve got a clear picture immediately of the strong verbal male.

She was aware that these strong verbal males would not fit her needs for friendship, love, or any enduring relationship. But she was stimulated by them and enjoyed the sexual feeling she had when she was near them. Eve summarized how she recognized the men who excited her sexually:

1. They do things easily for and to other persons.
2. They present a clearcut image of themselves; they are really there—you know it and they know it.
3. They look good in any style clothes.
4. They hold themselves well, walk and talk easily, and move gracefully.
5. They are "in touch" with things—how they work, and what to do when they break down.
6. You get the feeling that they know just what to do with you sexually without saying a word.

Occupation a clue to verbals

Eve and Karen were attracted sexually to aggressive men, and also admired their ability to cope with and understand the outer world. Eve had come to learn that these kind of men tended to get into certain kinds of occupations. This was not true in every case, but she found occupation to be a fairly reliable clue as to what kind of person a man might be.

Eve found that airplane pilots, military officers, engineers, lawyers, architects, politicans, and large business firm executives tended to be strong verbal men. (Not always, as noted before, do men in these occupations have strong verbal personalities. Many verbals are incompetent in their dealings with the outer world, and some anomics drift into these occupations.)

But Eve found that the successful men in these and similar occupations were usually verbals who attracted her sexually and had her admiration for being able to do things. But she knew that these men were "no good" for her; frequently she disliked them intensely, realizing they brought out her very worst traits in addition to her sexuality. She felt the verbals often were cruel, lacked real feeling for people, and seemed to enjoy hurting others. While this was sexually exciting, it did not allow for development of deeper bonds of love or friendship, or even for casual caring.

Eve kept verbal men at a distance with her "role for verbals." She made sure that there was at least one other person around as protection for herself. If she were "trapped" with a verbal male, she knew that she would follow the passive sexual female pattern unless there were a third party present to block the dynamic, to change this deadly diad into a triad to safe interaction.

Bryan and Cheryl: A third example

A description of anomics who dealt successfully with sex appears in chapter 6, in the case of Bryan and Cheryl. Bryan was a nonaggressive anomic male and Cheryl an aggressive anomic female. They fit one another very closely in their sexual and other behavior. This fit would probably have been equally successful if the tendencies were reversed, with Bryan an aggressive and Cheryl the nonaggressive anomic.

Bryan and Cheryl both liked things done to them. Bryan (nonaggressive anomic) did not masturbate often, feeling that it was unhealthy and that sex with a woman was more proper. When he was very young, two neighborhood boys his age introduced him to oral sex and, during a short period of a month or so, repeated the experience on several occasions. He enjoyed this but was frightened and felt guilty for years about the incidents.

Aggressive anomic Cheryl discovered masturbation when she was about nine. She felt guilty about it and thought she was different from others, but continued the practice through the years, keeping it a secret with an "oh-well, so-what, that's-the-way-I-am" attitude. In sexual activity, Cheryl liked everything done to her with fervor. She was strongly attracted to verbals like Mac, who was her boy friend for two years before she met Bryan. But Cheryl realized how absolutely she was dominated by Mac in a slavelike relationship, and that she liked this in some ways. But she was unhappy because her needs for love, affection, and warmth were not being met. She felt that Mac might walk off at any moment with a casual, "Well, it's been fun." This frightened her. She was ready to abandon the relationship as soon as she found something better.

When she met Bryan, she noticed immediately he was more her kind of man. He didn't talk much about himself, and seemed to be somewhat lost in the outer world of persons, jobs, and events. He needed help, someone to stand with him and face the outer world. Most of all, he *wanted* help. He was not ashamed to want a girl in this way.

Early sexual experiences

Bryan and Cheryl had similar sexual experiences in their early years. An older cousin of Cheryl's, a verbal female, who occasionally slept in the same bed with her, had sexually stimulated Cheryl and talked her into returning the behavior. On one occasion, this cousin introduced Cheryl to oral sex, but the relationship ended when the cousin's family moved away. The latter incident, like Cheryl's solitary sex, was interpreted by her as just another way in which she was "kind of crazy" and different from other women. So, she avoided verbal women from then on, feeling they were distrustful and dangerous for her. She didn't give this too much thought because she was so strongly attracted to verbal males and delighted with the sexual experiences she had with them.

With anomic Bryan she found a safer, more fulfilling relationship. Bryan felt pleasure when things were done to him, and Cheryl was just aggressive enough sexually to find pleasure in doing things for him. She needed sex more often than Bryan and, because he cared for her, he was willing to satisfy her even when he didn't feel the same need.

Cheryl found that verbals completed their sexual activity too vigorously and quickly for her. She liked to linger and dally. Bryan did, too. She and Bryan could devote a whole day "tinkering" with sex, luxuriating in low-intensity sexual contact: eating, drinking, talking, and so on. Bryan didn't want to do this often, only now and then. And this was a great comfort for Cheryl. Most, if not all, the men she had known previously were not like this.

Bryan was the more passive partner in their sex. Cheryl determined the pace. Bryan enjoyed oral sex and Cheryl obliged because she liked to make him happy. Cheryl liked oral sex too, and Bryan complied. Neither one had a strong desire to perform oral sex; rather, each had a desire to be the recipient. Cheryl liked anal sex, but Bryan didn't, so this was not part of their sex life.

Cheryl had had sexual experiences with verbal males who took great pleasure in performing oral sex, and in other dominant sex behavior patterns. But Cheryl had never been aggressive toward a male, she had liked "to be done to."

Cheryl could recognize a nonaggressive anomic male like Bryan easily. He did not offer a strong male image of himself, or talk, or do things well. He was kind, warm, and sensitive. He was not too neat in his dress, and didn't make firm contact with objects or persons. And he was not sexually attractive to her.

But Cheryl had trouble distinguishing between an aggressive anomic male and a strong verbal male. Often they both seemed the same at first, and she would become involved before she realized that someone she thought was a sensitive aggressive anomic like herself was really a strong verbal. An aggressive anomic male can "put up a front," that is, adopt a social role that gives him the appearance of a verbal personality.

One of her former boy friends, for instance, appeared on the surface to be a strong verbal male. He wanted to possess Cheryl, to govern her life, take all her time, tell her what to do, make her his slave. But Cheryl soon realized that this was a role that didn't fit him. He was actually very sensitive and out of touch with the outer world. He didn't know how to do things such as get a new job and cope with persons.

Cheryl found that her best guide to finding good verbal male sexual partners was to look for men who were successful gamblers, good car mechanics and drivers, or good at earning money. This may seem too simple a yardstick for finding sexual partners, but it seemed to work well for anomic Cheryl. The aggressive anomic male who fooled her was not successful in any of the above ways, but it took her some time to find this out, and to comprehend the role presentation.

Anomic sex summarized

In summary, then, anomic sex success apparently is determined by two conditions: Sex is most satisfying when things are done *to* an anomic – this is most exciting sexually. An anomic must find the kind of person who can meet this need, the strong verbal personality who wants *to do sexual things to someone*. (I am describing the dominant tendency – what is most strongly sexually exciting. Anomics may also enjoy doing sexual things to their partners, but this is less exciting to them and not what best fulfills their need.)

Some of the dilemma is resolved when a person, in this case an anomic person, can recognize that he is anomic, and can learn to recognize the verbal. An anomic can be satiated sexually by a verbal, but seldom, if ever, by another anomic. A major problem is identifying just who is what in the anomic-verbal pattern of sexuality—who is verbal and who is anomic—and how this can be determined quickly.

Finding sex partners

Through experience, anomic persons may develop their own yardsticks or guidelines for finding sex partners. Eve relied on a man's occupation, and on his ability to act with confidence in a social gathering; but perhaps more importance was the "electricity" she felt when a verbal male touched her. Another aggressive anomic, Cheryl, developed her simple gambler-car buff-breadwinner yardstick for finding sexually satisfying males.

Weak anomics (like Jeanette and Karen) are passive sexually, and have a more direct guideline: The male has to be aggressive enough to overcome their fears of the outer world and to penetrate their sexual person. These anomics need to be "attacked." Les forcefully sought out Jeanette; he was strongly drawn to her passive, anomic behavior. He pressed ahead in spite of her defenses and they eventually enjoyed a strong sexual relationship.

Karen's husband Ron, a strong verbal, continued to follow a pattern of sexual attack with her. He took sex from her, and she was excited by this. His aggression fitted with her passiveness. Karen tended to identify as good sexual partners only those who were similar in their behavior to her husband, Ron. This was her only guideline for choosing satisfying sex partners.

Bryan had what may seem to be an unusual guideline for spotting good sexual partners for himself: He compared the women he met to certain female characters in the comic strip *Peanuts,* and he checked a woman's feelings about dogs and cats. Bryan realized he was attracted sexually to verbal girls, represented by Lucy and Peppermint Patty. And, he found that verbal women generally do not like dogs and frequently do like cats.

In a similar way, weak anomics Jeanette and Karen spotted verbal males by their resemblance to strong verbal male movie stars or public personalities. Jeanette depended on this more than Karen, who used her husband Ron as her best guide.

Now, persons change as a result of growth and integration. Eve, for example, was a weak anomic in her younger days, and as she became more integrated, more in touch with herself and the outer world, she evolved from a weak anomic personality to an aggressive anomic personality. Her sexual tastes were still very much the same – she was strongly drawn to the "hard" verbal male – but she found broader satisfaction sexually with a "soft" verbal male, because, for her, sex had grown to be interrelated with needs of feeling close and protected, and of understanding one another better. Eve would not change so much as to become a verbal herself. Her tendency to be under-integrated, to be absorbed more in her inner world than with her outer world, came with her genes, was part of her biological makeup. Like the color of her eyes, that tendency would not change.

Her sexual needs matured and she became a more integrated and balanced person. The closer she got to integration, the easier it became for her to fulfill her sexual needs with "soft" verbal Roger. Eve's taste in movie stars, for instance, changed. She became more sexually attracted to "soft" verbals, stars like Robert Mitchum and Cary Grant, whereas primarily, she had liked Burt Lancaster, Kirk Douglas, and Clark Gable, all "hard" verbals.

Tendencies may change in degree

Verbals do not stop being verbal, nor do anomics stop being anomic. But the degree of these different orientations may or may not change, depending on whether or not the person moves toward healthy integration. As Eve learned to handle her outer world, to cope with learning how to do things, and to adopt new roles as she found roles that fit her, she could satisfy her sexual needs with Roger.

Weak anomics Jeanette and Karen would probably never integrate themselves enough to go beyond their sexual need for strong verbals. Bryan and Cheryl had an excellent chance for an enduring and fulfilling sex life with one another, especially if Bryan got over his jealousy of Cheryl's previous affairs with other men.

Personality integration in sex does not mean moving from anomic to verbal, that is, from one thing to its opposite. Integration is moving toward a person's "center," where his *natural behavior* comes together (is integrated) with his *social behavior,* and where his inner world "connects up" with his outer world. Verbal or anomic tendencies are inherited, and each person differs in the degree of verbal or anomic tendency he possesses. The degree may change as personal growth occurs, but the dominant tendency does not change.

May: An aggressive anomic

I want to offer one more example of anomic sex before moving on to anomic friendship. It relates to a common source of frustration for anomic persons. May was a woman of thirty-two and an aggressive anomic. She was strongly drawn to very "hard" verbal males, but she feared them and could barely talk when she met one. She was not sexually interested in other males so had never experienced sexual intercourse and felt desperate about this. She had fantasies and daydreams about sex, and masturbated regularly.

May was not a pretty woman, but she had a good figure and was sexually attractive to males. Socially, she could get along well with very nonagressive anomic males. In social gatherings, she would seek out this kind of male and they enjoyed talking and sharing their respective inner worlds. But she usually chose a male so anomic that he almost had to be attacked before he "gave in" to sex. With such a man, the woman must do all the work in setting up the sexual encounter. May frequently ended up with a homosexual male, much to her chagrin and disappointment. She didn't understand why this happened and blamed herself for poor judgment. (Some weak anomic males become homosexual and are uneasy with women.) May had to learn to seek out a new type of male.

Whenever she went to a cocktail lounge or to a party, May had to work at overcoming her fear of the strong verbal male. She was more comfortable and could talk more easily with the anomic male, but she knew she would be a virgin the rest of her life unless she could get over her self-defeating tendency to flee to safe relationships. She aggressively met anomic males but they ended up going to art galleries or movies instead of developing a sexual relationship. May could spot verbal males: they talked well, did things easily, and coped with the outer world that frightened her so much. Perhaps they were not always competent, but the males she liked sexually were not afraid of the outer world, of defeat, or of competition or battle.

A possible solution

May had tried several times to overcome her fears of making contact with a verbal male who would fulfill her sexual needs. However, she kept saying no, and seemed so distressed that the men dropped the relationship in disgust. She finally decided to have someone arrange a sexual encounter for her. This might have been a path to sexual success. Once she broke through this fear-strewn barrier, she might find the courage to get her own partners!

May had a female friend who agreed to help her find a male and to set it all up for her, all arranged and agreed on so that there wouldn't be any devastating failures. But the friend had a sexual relationship with May, and wasn't too interested in finding May a male partner.

May's girl friend was a verbal, and they did not have a very active sexual relationship. Two or three times a month, or less, they wound up an afternoon or evening together with oral sex. This was nearly incidental to the relationship; they enjoyed talking and being out together. May gained sexual pleasure from her friend's aggressiveness, the typical anom-ic-verbal sexual pattern, which in this case was construed as friendship. But these two women did not really like each other as friends. They argued a good deal, and did not share similar inner or outer worlds.

The odds against successful anomic sex

Let me review the probable and potential numbers of persons who are anomic or verbal, since these quite different personalities are drawn to one another in the strongest sexual attraction. Anomics outnumber verbals by about three to one. (About one-fourth of the population is verbal, and the rest anomic.) The ratio is similar for each sex. But so many males have adopted what appears to be verbal personality behavior that it might seem that the majority of males are verbals. However, this is a result of pressure to adopt certain roles. Males are taught (and thought) to be more aggressive, more outer-world oriented than females are taught to be in their roles, which are largely passive in nature, and resemble anomic behavior.

My research indicates that in the number of persons with verbal personalities, there are as many females as males. (Perhaps slightly more males are verbal than females in the total population.) A lot of very "hard" verbal female personalities are hidden behind the artificial adopted roles prescribed by our culture.

Clinical evidence, data from many other sources, and my own observations, support the idea that the differences in numbers of anomic males and females, and verbal male and females, are not significant. In other words, about seventy percent of all females are anomics, and twenty percent are verbals. The missing ten percent in each category might be considered as integrated anomics or verbals who are not caught in the personality trap of sex.

In any case, there does not seem to be enough verbals to go around for the anomics who are attracted to them sexually. Perhaps this explains the seemingly undying need for sex movies, books, literature, and art of all kinds. There seems to be a universal fascination with things sexual, along with a sad sense of unfulfilled desires compelling and pushing onward for expression, now and throughout social history.

Anomics and friendship

If anomics have more difficulty than verbals in finding sexual partners, they do much better (at least have numbers on their side) in finding friendship. In the gestalt group described in an earlier chapter, the anomics came out much better than the verbals in the long run.

Verbal males Mac and Les became close friends. Mac lost anomic Cheryl as a sex partner when she turned to Bryan in a love relationship that included friendship and sex for both. Les gained a sexual partner in anomic Jeanette for a while, but this affair was doomed. Jeanette gained more from her relationship with Les than he did in that she found a deep sexual experience for the first time. This was her first sexual experience; she had never even masturbated. Les "turned her on," and, relatively speaking, she gained more from the start than he.

Anomics Bryan and Cheryl first became friends; next, this grew into love accompanied by sex, in that order. Also, Bryan, Cheryl, and Jeanette formed a strong triad friendship, anchored by the diad bond between Bryan and Cheryl. Not long after the group became active, these three began to do things together in between the group meetings. They went to a mission, for instance, where they got interested in repairing broken toys and old clothes, and once a week shared this common activity and occasional forays into other, more leisurely enjoyment.

Anomics Bryan, Jeanette, and Cheryl shared an absorption in their inner world of feelings and emotions. They understood one another and were not afraid to express their uncertainties, fears, and guilts. Each knew that while the other two might not feel the same, they would understand. This triad contained some common patterns. Weak anomic Jeanette was drawn in friendship to aggressive anomic Cheryl. Jeanette did not care for weak anomic Bryan as much as she cared for more aggressive anomic males, but there were none in this group. The weak anomic person, such as Jeanette or Bryan, makes his closest friendships with an aggressive anomic, such as Cheryl.

As noted earlier, individuals may change from being a weak anomic to an aggressive anomic as a result of experience and growth toward integrating their inner and outer worlds. Jeanette might learn that her most successful friendships were with persons similar to Cheryl, seek them out, develop into an aggressive anomic, and reach a state of balanced integration. The major difference between the weak and aggressive anomic is usually that the aggressive anomic has found roles that fit him successfully.

It is very difficult for a verbal to teach group ways of doing things (roles) to an anomic person. Their lines of communication are based in different worlds. Cheryl's mother was a verbal woman. She tried to teach Cheryl roles as she understood them, and although Cheryl tried hard, she couldn't relate to or identify with her mother. Cheryl was fortunate in that she had an anomic sister, much older, who was able to translate what she had learned to do. Cheryl learned most of her roles from her sister, not her mother. She and her sister were good friends. Her sister was a weak anomic, but still Cheryl learned more from her about how to do specific things than she did from her mother.

Cheryl's two roles

Early in life, Cheryl learned two roles that fit her. Her basic integrating role, the one that held her together and dominated her personality, was one of "I'm a pretty, sexy, fun-kind-of-girl and easy to get along with." Her second and less dominant role was one of "young girl friend to all." Both of these roles fit Cheryl, and she absorbed much of these roles into her genuine natural behavior. She laughed a lot, liked people, liked to be friends with others, and had many,

many friends, both male and female. She differed from other anomics in that her central role was based on her sexuality, and her secondary role was based on her desire for friendship. Generally, anomics adopt a central role of "being-a-friend" as their major and perhaps only role. Jeanette was a good example; she had one very weak role that fit her: "I'm a good friend but you have to make all the moves."

A major characteristic of anomics is that they create their personality around a friendship role. Anomics find each other everywhere, it seems, through these friendship roles which they have adopted as their way of coping with the outer world.

Friendship is foremost

Anomics do seem to have the strongest friendships, stronger than those between other personalities. An anomic without one or two close friends seems to be the unhappiest person in the world; an anomic can do without sex more easily than he can do without friends. Anomics tend to let friendship take the place of, or stand in for, other social bonds.

Bryan and Cheryl, although fairly well-matched sexually as weak and aggressive anomics, would probably drop much of their sexuality in later years to emerge as very good friends who happen to be married to one another. Weak anomic Karen had a great deal of trouble with "hard" verbal Ron because they were not friends. And she was not aggressive enough to go out and build close friendships with anomic males and females. She wanted Ron to change and be a friend too, not just a vigorous sexual partner.

Eve and Roger had a better marriage relationship because Eve (an aggressive anomic in contrast to Roger's soft verbal tendencies) was closer to Roger than Karen was to Ron, and could feel friendship with him in addition to a sexual bond. Being aggressive, Eve also had several other male and female friends, all anomics. She didn't try to make her marriage relationship stand in for her need for close friendship with other males or females.

As Eve became more integrated, and absorbed more of her roles as her own genuine behavior, her need for several close friendships diminished as she grew closer to Roger, and he to her. She still needed to share some of her inner fears and experiences with another anomic since she couldn't fully share them with Roger; not because he didn't care for her, but because he simply didn't understand how she felt.

Now, anomics cannot cope with too many friends at the same time. Aggressive Eve and several, but most anomics do not relate deeply to several persons at any given time. Anomics Jeanette, Karen, Cheryl, Eve, and Bryan are illustrative: They had to relate to a person as an individual, face-to-face, regularly, and with feeling, or the bond tended to fade out.

If anomics are in a group of more than two or three friends, they have trouble relating to any of them. The anomic triad of Cheryl, Jeanette, and Bryan was anchored in the diad bond between Cheryl and Bryan, both of whom accepted Jeanette as their friend. The anomic friendship pattern is strongest in diads, where the two can interact with just one another without the dynamic being hindered by one or more other persons.

Anomics have difficulty when they see too many friends too often. Aggressive anomics Eve and Cheryl each had many friends, but only one or two very close friends, whom they saw regularly in diad encounters (where there was just the two of them). "Two's company, three's a crowd" probably was coined by an anomic. And most likely it was a verbal who wrote "The more, the merrier!"

One-to-one relationships

The key to this tendency seems to be that the anomic cannot relate well to more than one person at a time. Anomics relate as self-to-person with others, regardless of the occasion, but do not have roles that allow them to relate formally to large numbers of persons within any social situation. The verbal is different; he can relate to this outer world of persons, for he has adopted roles whereby this comes much more easily. As will be seen, the verbal's friendship patterns are quite different from the anomic's.

The friendship role for the anomic seems to be the keystone to his happiness. Friendship apparently is the first step to deep love with another person. This feeling of friendship is the central underlying driving force of the anomic, who is so absorbed in his inner world of feelings, and friendship then grows into the full emotional response of love. This requires a close self-to-person relationship, and is necessary if the anomic is to become an integrated person.

Anomic friendship patterns

Anomics develop strong, close friendships with one another. Anomics may be friends and also have sex, or love, or even marriage, but friendship must come first for them to find success in these others.

Two weak anomics (such as Jeanette and Karen) probably would not get along too well. They would not be able to organize their relationship sufficiently as they have such weak links to the outer world of how to do things and get around. Neither Jeanette nor Karen drove cars, knew how to handle money, or could get from one place to another by bus. They might have felt a closeness to each other, and they would have understood each other very well. But that was no guarantee that they would have liked each other. In fact, each might have seen too much of herself in the other, and therefore would have felt uncomfortable in a close relationship. Both would have developed close friendships with persons like Cheryl and Eve, who were aggressive anomics, and who had discovered roles that fit them and helped them cope with the outer world.

While deep hatred often arises between verbals and anomics, there seems to be a special kind of dislike that sometimes happens between weak anomics. Anomics tend to blame themselves for what happens to them, but weak anomics will at times blame other weak anomics for their own difficulties. So again, whether male or female, the best friendship pattern for the weak anomic is to build bonds with the more aggressive anomic, male or female. It is difficult to estimate the number of people in these categories because the weak anomic may grow and change, that is, become more aggressive, as he finds roles that fit him and absorbs this role behavior as his own.

Two aggressive anomics make good friends, perhaps the best friends of all. An aggressive-weak anomic combination makes for good friendship too, and perhaps results in a better sexual pattern. Cheryl and Eve would probably have been close friends, but not Karen and Jeanette. Weak anomic Bryan and Cheryl were good friends with adequate sexual contact, but this probably wouldn't have happened if Bryan had taken up with Jeanette.

Eve and Karen might have been good friends, as one was an aggressive anomic and the other a weak anomic. The slenderest of relationships is formed between two weak anomics; the friendship is tenuous and is generally blown apart by the first strong wind. Weak anomics should seek aggressive anomics as close friends; aggressive anomics should seek either weak or other aggressive anomics as friends. Neither should waste time trying to be friends with a verbal. Verbals form very poor friendships with anomics, leading them always into a pattern of dominance and submission to the verbals' needs.

Being together important to anomics

There seems to be another major characteristic of anomic friendship behavior. Anomics Bryan, Cheryl, and Jeanette enjoyed doing things together. It didn't matter so much what they did, the important thing was that whatever the activity, working at the mission or going to a show, the enjoyment came from their *being together*.

In contrast, verbals have friendships based on activity. For instance, verbals Les and Mac had a friendship which rested on their common interest in cars. They liked to tinker with engines. If it weren't for this, or for some other activity in the outside world of doing things, they probably would not have become friends. This is a significant difference: Verbals share an activity while anomics share one another.

Thus, the anomic person should not try to establish a friendship based on what the other person is doing, whether a job, hobby, or interest. Anomic Jeanette spent a lot of time swimming at the beach. She went swimming not because she liked it, but because she was lonely and didn't know what else to do with herself. After she met Bryan and Cheryl, she stopped going to the beach to swim. Again, it was *being together* that was the basis for the anomic friendship, not the activity being done.

Recognizing very weak anomics

Very weak anomics are easy to recognize. At times, Karen and Jeanette seemed to flutter into a room. They dropped things, and they tended to get hysterical and fall apart in a crisis. They had *too many feelings* swirling around inside. They didn't express themselves well. They had trouble with cigarette lighters and machines of any kind. Once, when Karen was driving her car, the radiator ran low on water and the engine overheated. She was surprised to learn that water wasn't "permanently installed" at the factory!

Karen would clean her bathroom carefully in preparation for guests, then forget to put out a single towel; or would serve a meal and forget part of the main course. The disorganization of behavior is readily seen in the weak anomic, and less easily seen in the aggressive anomic by persons who meet them. Aggressive anomics Eve and Cheryl adopted strong roles that fit them, and had absorbed some of this behavior as their own genuine, natural selves. They had strong friendship roles and could talk well with others in these roles. Their wife and mother roles were enhanced by these strong friendship roles, but were secondary to them, and supported by the stronger friendship pattern underneath.

Aggressive anomics (like Eve and Cheryl) frequently are

mistaken for verbals because they seem to offer a firm image because of their outer behavior. They seem sure of themselves when in their friendship roles or in secondary wife-mother roles. The key to recognizing them as anomics, though, is found in being around them for a while. They do not like to relate to others in large groups. They prefer the one-to-one relationship, or a group of three. When in a group of four or more persons, they tend to relate to a single person at a time. When Eve and Roger were with another couple for an evening, Eve tended to relate to **just one** of the persons they were with, or she would talk **or respond** mostly to Roger.

For anomics, a three-person (triad) dynamic is about the upper limit for relating closely with other persons at any given time. Their role behavior of personality does not seem to allow them to reduce their awareness of what other persons are doing to the point where they can understand what is going on. Bryan, Eve, Karen, and Cheryl tended to lose track of the conversation when they were with four or more persons. Anomics tend to get only bits and pieces of the varied happenings between persons, including themselves, in large groups.

Anomic friends, then, want to be together rather than to do something together, and then only in very small informal groups of two or three persons. Five-person groups seem to be the upper limit for anomics; add more persons and they lose the person-to-person feeling. This makes the artificial groups (such as groups that form on sensitivity weekends, marathons, and the like) especially devastating for the anomic. If an anomic tries to relate openly to several persons at a time, he increases his feelings of alienation and gets more and more out of touch with himself, the very reverse of his reason for being in the group.

In summary, weak anomics do not form good friendships among themselves. A weak anomic and an aggressive anomic can be good friends. The best anomic friendships are possible between two aggressive anomics. This is possible, but not inevitable.

Anomics do not make friendships with verbals. What may

seem to be a friendship between an anomic and verbal is usually a sharing of an activity or a role relationship. For instance, verbal Mac felt that Cheryl was his friend because she liked to go on long rides in his car with him. He liked to get out and race his car. Cheryl asked to go riding with Mac because she was attracted to him sexually and wanted to be with him, whatever they were doing.

In another instance, verbal Ron felt that Karen was his friend because she was his wife and not because he liked her as a person. Actually, he didn't like her; he wanted her to change almost completely and be another kind of a person. So, anomics may seem to have verbal friends, but they are really sharing an activity or a role relationship with a verbal.

Anomics and love

Perhaps the biggest difference between anomics and verbals is in the love relationship. Anomic persons can build stronger friendships than verbals, and thus can build deeper love for one another. The verbal has a very hard time knowing what love is, or experiencing it.

Anomics Bryan and Cheryl liked one another first, then became friends, then intimate friends, then fell in love as the full range of various personal needs for each was answered by the other person. Verbals do not make this deep, close contact with another person easily. Love is a bleak mystery for the verbal, and the anomic attempting to build a love relationship with the verbal suffers great frustration. As may be seen later, two verbals handle this better, but love is still a mystery for them. (This kind of difference may be seen in solutions for man's ills: the anomic says man needs to love more; the verbal says man needs to correct his behavior through external controls or self-discipline!)

Anomic Karen and verbal Ron could never have found love with one another. Nor could anomic Jeanette and verbal Les, nor verbal Mac and aggressive anomic Cheryl. Verbals are not in close touch with their inner world of feelings, which are crucial for love. Love is an emotion that arises out of feelings that come from inner needs for warmth, protection, security, closeness, and so on. When the inner needs are met and satisfied by another person, love is possible and likely.

On a scale of "sex-friendship-love," the anomic finds his splendor in *love*. The verbal shines in *sex,* diminishing in ability in friendship, then love. The anomic has weak sexuality, growing in strength in *friendship* and is strongest in love with another.

Anomics, like Bryan and Cheryl, feel alive only when they are in love. Verbals, like Ron or Mac or Les, feel alive only when they have a strong sexual contact with another person. Both are "turning on" in their respective worlds. Gross frustration results for both anomics and verbals if they are not aware of their personal needs when they come together in their relationships with one another.

The agony can be sharp, as for instance with Cheryl. She spent much of her life strongly attracted sexually to verbals like Mac, but was unable to find love in the thrust of his penis or the touch of his lips — excitement and even ecstasy — but not love. Cheryl experienced intercourse with many men before she met Bryan, and with an inner wisdom she found her way to him. She taught Bryan to do the things verbals did to her sexually that had always excited and pleased her so much.

Cheryl still had instant sexual feeling for a strong verbal male when she met one. But she taught Bryan to be aggressive sexually. They learned to fit one another. Cheryl no longer confused her sexual desires with her search for love. Sex was secondary with Bryan and Cheryl.

They were good friends and loved each other. They worked out their sex needs. With love, both would become more and more integrated over the years. Their sexual needs and inclinations would not change, but *the manner* in which these needs were met would change with integration.

As Bryan integrated himself, he would become more and more sexually aggressive. It takes time for anomics to work out what to do to satisfy each other's deep sexual needs. But sex between anomics and verbals doesn't have to be "worked at," for the attraction is fundamental and is buttressed from the start by passion that casts aside barriers and finds its own way through individual differences.

Anomics have to be careful about how they find love relationships. They make friends quickly, but they tend to respond too soon to one another and try to make a friendship become a love relationship when they don't feel that deeply yet. Anomics have to be friends before they can be in love, and frequently they say they are in love but mean they have a good friend.

Anomics know that they are in love with another person when they don't want that person to change in any way. When Bryan met Jeanette, for instance, he liked her on sight, but he wanted her to be more aggressive after he had known her awhile. He wanted her to be a little different. He was not satisfied with her the way she was.

When Bryan met Cheryl, he basically liked everything about her. He didn't want her to change anything: her looks, or her way of talking, acting, or thinking. He didn't like her sexual past, and didn't want her running around with other men after he met her. And he was bothered sometimes when he thought about all of her other sexual partners. She was a little too aggressive for him in other ways, too. But he didn't want to change her. That is the key for an anomic to recognize when he (or she) is in love. If the other person has to change to become something else as a condition of "love," then love is not there, and perhaps it's only friendship.

Successful anomic sex, friendship, and love

The most successful sexual relationship for the anomic is one with a verbal. This seems true for several reasons, the most significant being the deep matching of "missing parts" in the creative sexual act between them. It was with verbals that anomics Cheryl, Jeanette, Karen, Eve, and Bryan probably had the most satisfying, exciting, completely sexual relationships, ones that gratified their inner sexual needs.

Anomics want and need things done to them by others; this is a way to link their inner world of feelings and emotions with the outer world of other persons. It seems that the only creative relationship between anomics and verbals is sexual. Anomics tend to be masochistic and passive sexually, and verbals tend to be aggressive and sadistic sexually, a complementary fit.

The most successful friendship relationship for the anomic is with another anomic. Especially successful is friendship between a weak and an aggressive anomic. Two weak anomics make very poor friends. They have trouble maintaining routine friendship patterns of doing things together.

The most successful anomic love relationship also is with another anomic. Love comes best between two aggressive anomics. The enduring, deep linking of the inner world of feelings and emotions is possible here as in no other "match" of kinds of persons.

Aggressive anomics may not win the battle of material wealth or of coping expertly with the outer world, but they do have the potential of deep, if not deepest, contact with one another. Anomics may lose the battle of sex, but they gain ground in their ability to be friends, and finally are the victors in love.

10

Verbals and Sex, Friendship, and Love

Frank, a young physician of twenty-eight, is married to Theodora (Teddy), who is also twenty-eight and a physician. They met in medical school, were married within two weeks, graduated together in the same class, and set up practice in different offices. He was a general practitioner, and she a pediatrician. Both graduated near the top of their class.

Frank was a big, blond, masculine man who moved with the grace of an athlete. Teddy was a tall, slender blonde woman who also moved with ease and grace. They were handsome persons who chose each other partly for this reason, but mostly because both were strong verbal personalities.

They admired and respected each other as capable and intelligent persons who shared a common goal and an understanding of the outside world of action, achievement, and social success. But neither was very sophisticated sexually. Both had very limited sexual experience before they married; both had experienced sex with others when they were in their teens. But neither had taken much time away from their studies for any other activities.

Sex between Frank and Teddy was a quick burst of energy and technique. They studied the best available medical manuals, and their sexual activity was academic, a masterpiece of gymnastics, wherein they carefully and systematically did things to each other. They probed and pounded, bit, hugged and kissed each other clinically, employing what they understood to be the best techniques. It resembled a carefully ritualized battle where blood is drawn to end the contest.

They did not understand why there was dissatisfaction in their feelings for one another, especially after one of these sexual bouts. They did not talk about it; instead, they gradually worked into other sexual patterns with other persons.

They had a friend I'll call Craig. He was a successful attorney who handled a malpractice suit for Frank, which led to the personal relationship. Craig was forty, and a "soft" verbal. He had a wife, Joanna, a weak anomic, whom he met and married at college. Joanna was thirty.

Craig was homely, but it was an attractive, masculine homeliness. Joanna had the dark, wispy beauty of a pageant queen. The couple revelled in their sexual delight with one another. They met at a college party and left within fifteen minutes to spend the rest of their first evening "in bed." They say they fell in love at first sight, but actually, they fell in love with sex.

These two couples, Frank and Teddy, and Craig and Joanna, became involved with one another, and their lives were intermingled.

Let me describe verbals again briefly before going on.

How to recognize verbals

Frank and Teddy were "hard" verbal personalities. Craig was a "soft" verbal personality. There are differences between the "hard" and "soft" verbal, but there are some fundamental similarities, too. Verbals, such as Frank, Craig, and Teddy, learn how to do things far more easily than anomics, like Joanna. They easily make good grades in school, learn how to drive, keep budgets, figure math problems, play games, organize their lives, and plan ahead. It is easier for them to learn new skills, adopt new behavior, understand do-it-yourself projects, and figure out how things fit together.

Verbals are better at coordinating themselves with the outside world of action and doing things. They take less time than anomics to accomplish whatever they do. They are not necessarily more creative or competent than aggressive anomics, but they do things more quickly, assume the lead more readily, and are willing to take the first step, even if it's wrong.

Verbals have many roles for meeting most social situations. Their roles may be too rigid, and frequently are. For instance, they tend to greet all strangers in the same way, with hand out and a ready smile. They tend to organize a simple picnic with as much intensity as a month's trip. They are better at cards, at puzzles, and at most things that involve competition with other persons or with gambling odds. They usually have a better memory for facts and events. They have a better sense of time, of compass direction, of up or down, of where things exist in space, and of depth perception.

The principal trait

But the main trait of verbals seems to be that they want to do things *to* another person or object, rather than have things done to them. As an example, Teddy lighted Frank's cigaret as often as he did hers. It was a matter of who had the lighter. And Teddy didn't usually wait for Frank to open a door for her.

Verbals have many roles for manners in eating, walking, talking, and doing things with others. They prefer formal over informal behavior. They tend to by-pass their inner feelings or emotions as unnecessary and a sign of weakness.

Because they are uneasy with the concept of love, verbals would rather call it sex. They are drawn to violence in games or other relationships; they may not be violent themselves, but they are attracted to violence in stories or films. They enjoy man's violent struggles with the elements, with hurricanes and earthquakes, and in mountain climbing: man pitted against the world and winning! They tend to adopt roles where this struggle is personified or personalized.

As noted earlier, verbals are in charge nearly everywhere. They become leaders and tend to get into occupations where leadership is required, where human behavior is organized and structured in complex role relationships. They become lawyers and doctors, engineers, foremen, executives, managers, politicians—leaders of all kinds. They may and frequently do lead badly, but they lead.

"Hard" verbals are easily recognized. They talk well, do things well, and learn things quickly. They do things easily for other persons, have ready social roles and are at ease in any gathering. Cerebral, logical, and reasonable, they punish ignorance in others with well-chosen words. They want to do things to others, correct behavior, and organize them; and they know how to use words to express how these things are to be done.

Craig was a soft verbal who didn't talk much; he was silent much of the time. But he was a "silent verbal" who was always thinking, and he spoke softly and with great firmness when he did talk. His silences terrified Joanna because she hadn't the slightest idea what he was thinking about. Craig was not a trial lawyer, but he could be devastatingly competent in a courtroom because he so carefully prepared his excellent briefs. Having a remarkable memory for detail, he silently organized, sorted, and filed his thoughts in an orderly sequence.

Verbals and sex

When Frank, Teddy, Criag, and Joanna met together socially, they chose an activity to be shared—tennis. Frank, Craig, and Teddy, all verbals, were comfortable with one another immediately because they shared the same interest in tennis, but Joanna felt left behind because she didn't feel close to the new couple as persons. This is a common verbal-anomic difference.

But all four persons in this group shared something else:

an underlying dissatisfaction with themselves and with their relationship with their mate. Frank and Teddy puzzled over why they didn't feel better about their gymnastic sex life, and Craig and Joanna wondered why they had such a good sex life but didn't feel close in any other way.

Frank and Teddy felt that they had a colorful sex relationship, which was even mischievous at times. They were delighted with one experience that occurred shortly after they got married. Teddy sat on Frank's lap during a large party and they had intercourse under the cover of her skirt, without anyone realizing (apparently) what was happening. People would approach and attempt to have the casual cocktail party conversations, while Teddy grinned a little in response now and then, and Frank tried to talk evenly and maintain a fixed smile.

This was their most exciting sexual experience. Much later they told a few friends who were at that party, but no one believed it. They remembered that Teddy had sat on Frank's lap for an hour or so, and that both had drinks in their hands, and were talking and joking and laughing with others in the room – part of the party all the time.

Both Teddy and Frank were a trifle ashamed of how much that long-ago act stimulated them. Each recreated this sexual memory to heighten stimulation whenever they had sex. They did not understand why this was necessary. Neither wished to discuss it with the other, but each wondered whether the other was using this old experience in the same way.

Both were taking their strongest sexual memory and reintegrating it with current behavior each time they had sexual activity. This is a very common dynamic. Both felt that they were doing something to another – Frank to Teddy and Teddy to Frank – and that the *presence of other people* reinforced the interchange of sexuality.

Both were active sexually and used sex in an aggressive, athletic, competitive sort of way. They looked forward to it each day, and even when tired from their work, were drawn to end the day in sexual games. Still, there was lingering dissatisfaction with one another which they could not find words to express.

Craig and Joanna had a different pattern. Craig was the more active; he wanted sex more often and more quickly than Joanna, who preferred to take more time, and not have sex so often. Once involved in sexual activity with Craig, however, she enjoyed herself and the experience. She preferred oral sex more than any other method, and Craig liked to oblige her. This was their closest match. But he liked any sort of sexual activity and she delighted in whatever he did to her. She was in a glow for hours after a long session with Craig.

Craig got his peak enjoyment doing things *to* Joanna, and she got peak enjoyment having things done to her. Craig sometimes was too rough and hurt her, but that excited her too. Here is the verbal-anomic sexual match, a complementary fit.

But Craig and Joanna, like Frank and Teddy, had a lingering dissatisfaction. And this was the emotional state these couples were in when they met. None had ever strayed from their mates to other persons, and each felt that his or her own marriage was on solid ground. Both couples felt that since their sex life was the center of their marriage, their marriage should be a success.

But verbals Frank and Teddy were friends, and did not love deeply. They had a very strong friendship but were not sexually matched for the deeper sex relationship that verbals may have with anomics. Verbal Craig and anomic Joanna were sexually matched, but they were not friends, nor did they love one another.

Verbals and group sex

Frank and Craig bought a vacation home together, more as an investment at the time than as a retreat. The cabin was on property near a lake in ski country. Inevitably, the two couples planned a long-weekend winter vacation. Frank, Teddy, and Craig liked to ski, and Joanna liked to get away from the city and relax amid the scenery.

On the way to the cabin, the couples realized they liked each other very much; at least Frank, Teddy, and Craig felt a strong bond. Joanna liked Frank and Teddy, but she didn't understand them. They seemed impersonal so much of the time, so glib and smooth. She liked them because Craig liked them, and she trusted his judgment.

There was a sexual explosion the first evening at the cabin. After much drinking, Frank told Joanna he wanted to talk with her alone and took her to one of the bedrooms. Craig smiled at her and nodded encouragement. Craig and Teddy said nothing and also went to a bedroom at the other side of the cabin.

Joanna was very drunk and confused. Up to the last moment, she thought Frank wanted only to talk. She fought as Frank began his sexual advances, but he pinned her down. Ultimately she stopped fighting and was caught up in Frank's sexual fury. Joanna had never experienced such intense, driving, extremely exciting pain-pleasure even in her wildest moments with Craig. Frank didn't do anything so different, but he did it with more excitement and vigor.

Frank had never had sex with an anomic woman before, and it was a most satisfying and exhilarating experience as Joanna responded to his need. Craig was a "soft" verbal, and Joanna had never experienced the sexual ruthlessness of a "hard" verbal like Frank. Her body ached for hours after this session with Frank. Frank apologized for his roughness; he hadn't intended to be so rough.

The aftermath

It was an exhilarating experience for both Frank and Joanna. But this evening quickly turned into a disaster for all of them. While Frank was leisurely winding down from the high passion of an hour or so, Joanna opened her eyes and saw her husband, Craig, leaning against a set of drawers near the door, naked, drink in hand, watching them in the faint light. Joanna gasped and broke away from Frank. Craig left the room without a word or sound.

Frank got up and went out to the big room where Craig and Teddy sat, exhausted from their own experience. Teddy got up and went in to Joanna with full drinks in hand. Teddy patted and stroked Joanna, who seemed to be in shock. Teddy began kissing and caressing her, then performed oral sex on her. Joanna allowed Teddy to do this without protest, and was even more deeply shocked with herself. She had enjoyed Frank and she enjoyed Teddy. She had never felt so sexually satisfied, but so full of shame, guilt, and stark fear. Her world had shattered and slipped out from under her. Teddy knew something was wrong and left her quietly. Joanna got dressed, went out to Craig's station wagon, and drove back to town.

After Joanna left, Craig, Frank, and Teddy drank some more, much more. Craig had never had intercourse with a woman like Teddy and was in sexual shock from the things she had taught him in a short hour's session. Teddy was not impressed at all with Craig, and preferred Frank, her "hard" verbal husband.

But Teddy was excited about her brief act with Joanna, although she realized that she really liked only men, and disliked Joanna as a person. This puzzled Teddy. And after more drinking, the three joined in a triad of sex, venting the sexual excitement generated from their earlier contacts with one another. It was difficult for them to find ways, it all seemed so awkward: two men trying to do something to one woman at the same time and only getting in each other's way. This experience was an emotional disaster for all three. Finally, they dressed and drove back to town in Frank's car. It was surprising how quickly they sobered up although they had consumed a great deal of whiskey.

Frank and Craig revived their friendship later on. But Joanna divorced Craig. She couldn't get over the image of Craig standing at the door watching her.

Frank and Teddy slowly worked their way through their own personal corridors. He changed after his experience with anomic Joanna, with whom he had a tremendous sexual fit. He discovered that his office nurse, who had been with him for some time, had similar anomic tendencies. So he turned to her; a sexual relationship developed to the satisfaction of both of them.

Teddy decided to have a child and promptly got pregnant. There was no thought of divorce, nor was the vacation house experience ever mentioned. Sex between Frank and Teddy became less pressured, and they began to enjoy one another in ways that they hadn't previously.

Variations in verbal sex

Sex between verbals and anomics is not always so exciting as the foregoing examples might indicate. Frequently there are wide variations. Perhaps a good example of this is revealed in the sexual history of Marcia, a woman of forty who had been married to a verbal, Gene, for several years.

Gene was forty-five and a "soft" verbal. He was a successful writer of technical manuscripts for science journals and business firms. Marcia had become an aggressive anomic, but only in the past few years. For most of her early life she had been a weak anomic with no basic role behavior that fit her, but she had always been strongly attracted sexually to the verbal male. She developed friendships with anomic males and anomic females, but her sex life was confined to the verbal male.

This is how she described her sexual experiences with verbal males:

"My first two lovers were not satisfactory. I felt absolutely nothing. My third lover really turned me on. I really have to think hard to find differences in the men. All were about the same age. The first two were from the lower middle class. I see now that this made a difference with me. Brad, the third lover, was from an upper middle-class background. All three seemed very masculine men with good personalities.

"I think one difference was that Brad, my third lover, took time with me. We spoke very little. When he first started with me, he put his hand on my abdomen and that really turned me on. Then he kissed me on the lips, with his hand still on my abdomen. Then he moved his hands slowly over my body.

"Everything Brad did was very calm, competent, sophisticated. He never acted differently than this. I felt very sensuous and sophisticated. When he put his penis in me, I just lay there. I didn't know enough to raise my legs. I had a climax—my first in my life.

"Then we smoked a cigaret. Then he started all over again. I never felt the need to ask him if I was doing anything wrong. He never told me to do anything different. When the evening was over, I didn't feel anything for him, except that he was a great lover. I thought I would have warm feelings for him, but I didn't. I went to bed with him once more before I met Gene. When Brad called me for the third time, I told him I had met someone and was calling it off with him. Brad said to call him if I changed my mind.

"After I married Gene, once he put his hand on my abdomen and I really got turned on. That night, for the first time, I felt that Gene had looked and inspected my body for the first time in our marriage. And I was really turned on."

A case of straightforward sex

This is a case where anomic Marcia's most vivid sexual experience, and what excited her sexually, was simple. straightforward, unadorned sex with a verbal male. No frills, no elaborate preparations, just straight verbal-anomic sex between two persons who were deeply attracted by the direct sexual needs of each other. Marcia did not have complicated sexual needs, nor did Brad. Both found great pleasure and excitement in the sexual joining of man and woman, carefully, slowly, and without embellishment.

There are elements of this that warrant notice. I believe that this was very close to a spiritual experience. Nowhere else have I found persons integrating their inner and outer worlds in a single creative act so easily and quickly.

This is not to say that if this occurs, the verbal and the anomic will get along in their day-to-day lives. Not at all. If

Marcia and Brad had tried to stay together in a marriage, it probably would not have worked. I do mean to say that the sexual act between the verbal and the anomic has the impact of joining their respective natures in ways that no other combination of verbal or anomic behavior can. In this case, they came together in a direct, straightforward manner, at a point in time when each had a need that could be fulfilled easily by the other. This matching of inner and outer needs resembles the spiritual reflex, the linking of the inner and outer worlds of a person who lacks awareness of one or the other. When this happens, it is a sexual and spiritual fit. Most verbal and anomic sex has this undertone. It is just more clear when it is expressed so purely.

Let me return to Gene and Marcia. Gene, although a verbal, did not have a strong sex drive and he liked to do a variety of different things to Marcia. He liked oral sex, and occasionally anal sex. Marcia enjoyed these variations, especially oral sex. She did not care to reciprocate, however, so this was not part of their sexual pattern.

A characteristic of males

Marcia enjoyed having things done *to* her, and Gene enjoyed doing them. But, as described in her statement earlier, Marcia didn't need sexual variety. This points to one of the characteristics of verbal (and other) males. Gene needed a variety of sexual stimulation before he got excited sufficiently and, once reaching orgasm, his sexual need was diminished and gratified until the next time. Perhaps the most important difference then (from Marcia's viewpoint) between her sexual needs and those of verbal males, is revealed in her description of Brad, who was deliberate and gentle, and who gave her a sense of sexual completion.

Gene found sexual satisfaction with Marcia, but he realized he did not give her a sense of completion. This was revealed in several ways, but mainly in that Marcia never pressed him for sex. And he knew that the other women he had been with were far more excited with him than Marcia ever had been. Otherwise, Gene and Marcia had an interesting relationship, as may be seen in later paragraphs.

Successful verbal sex

The most successful sex for verbals comes when they have an anomic partner (as in the example of verbal Craig and anomic Joanna). Their respective inner and outer sexual needs complement and match one another. It seems that a major way in which the verbal, caught up in the outer world, can get in touch with the inner world is through the sexual act with an anomic who is absorbed in the inner world of emotions.

The next best sex pattern for verbals is that between a hard and a soft verbal, illustrated by soft verbal Craig and hard verbal Teddy. This matching didn't come off well in the group sex both were involved in, but given time, Craig could become a better fit for Teddy (although she didn't think so that particular evening). Teddy was responding to a preference for her husband, hard verbal Frank, in other than sexual matters; it wasn't that Craig was "not as good as Frank." Verbal sex between hard verbals, like Teddy and Frank, is the least successful combination when compared with the other combinations.

Teddy and Frank were like two competing athletes, one of whom must outdo the other and win. Sex was almost a superficial experience for them, as they were both relating to what they were doing to each other, and not to what was being done to them. There would not have been this intensity of competitiveness if one had been a softer verbal, less captured by outer behavior, and more integrated in an inner response to sex.

But even a hard and a soft verbal have more difficulty finding satisfaction with each other than, say, a weak anomic and an aggressive anomic. The verbal is usually far more active sexually than the anomic in terms of variety and amount of sex desired. But, this is a general statement, with many exceptions in individual behavior. This is indicated in the wide variety of needs and behavior described in the various examples in the preceeding pages.

Verbals and friendship

Friendship for verbals is based upon a sharing of roles in their personalities. This is not a self-to-person friendship such as two anomics develop with one another, but a sharing of things done together. It is not just being together, which is the basis of the anomic bond.

For example, Frank and Teddy had a strong verbal friendship bond based upon their mutual respect and admiration for what the other had achieved in his outer world. Both had strong roles as husband and wife, as physicians, party-goers, intellectuals, informed citizens, athletes, civic-minded and concerned members of a community, helpers of humanity, and as skillful leisure companions. They had all of these roles in common, in which they related to one another and understood what each other was doing. They did not have long, intimate talks about their feelings or emotions; both felt this was almost irrelevant to the more important outer-world things.

Teddy organized her life in roles, just as did Frank. When she cooked breakfast (or any other meal), she had a specific dress, apron, and other things to wear. She organized her kitchen with expertness and used time-saving appliances. Frank beamed with pride when he watched her in her cooking role. He got pleasure when she served her usual, well-prepared meals, done just right and on time.

And Teddy, in turn, delighted in relating to Frank in his masculine roles, such as the hunter with gun. He took her with him on hunting trips occasionally, and taught her to shoot. She was a good shot, nearly but not quite as good as Frank. And it was always a contest enjoyed by both. She wanted to win and so did he.

Whatever their activity — skiing, sex, eating, driving, going to parties, reading at home — they had a durable set of roles in which to relate to one another, and in which both found great comfort. Their sex life changed after the cabin affair, but they both created new roles to handle this situation, to suppress their inner emotional responses that might have interfered with their strong verbal friendship pattern.

Teddy knew Frank was having an affair with his anomic nurse, and understood why. She was getting a little weary of their sexual bouts, anyway. Her baby had given her the first close touch with her inner world of feelings that she had ever experienced. She recognized the sexual undertones of her needs, the intimate touching and warmth of human contact, that were being satisfied with her baby. The baby softened this hard verbal woman, and she enjoyed a fuller and richer life.

Verbal friendship is based on doing something together

The essential pattern here was that hard verbals Frank and Teddy had a relationship anchored in their friendship with one another. This friendship consisted of relating to one another *in what was being done together,* and not in the anomic pattern *of just being together* regardless of what's being done. Teddy and Frank related to each other in their outer worlds with their personality of roles.

Now, soft verbal Craig and weak anomic Joanna were not friends. Joanna could not relate to Craig in any of his roles: husband, lover, organizer, masculine man, or lawyer. When their sexual bond was shattered, they had nothing to fall back on in their relationship. Had Joanna been an aggressive anomic, perhaps they could have developed friendship roles that might have helped save their relationship.

This brings us to Gene and Marcia as examples. Soft verbal Gene and aggressive anomic Marcia had created several roles of friendship between them in which they could find a fit. Marcia, for instance, never could develop a friendship with the verbal males she chose as sex partners, but she did have friendship roles with anomic males. So, she had had some practice, before she married Gene, in friendship-with-a-male roles. Her female friends also were mostly anomics. Marcia intensely disliked verbal females.

Gene and Marcia's marriage floundered for the first few years. It was as if they were underwater and couldn't talk or reach one another. Gene had trouble relating to Marcia because she had virtually no roles — sexual, housekeeping, social, or otherwise. He kept trying to find roles for himself in which he could relate to her, and he also tried to get her to change, and to adopt the roles he felt he could be most comfortable with.

Marcia kept trying to reach Gene in a warm person-to-person relationship, but she, too, was caught in the role trap. She wanted Gene to adopt certain roles to which she could relate easily. Because Gene didn't seem to want sex often with her, and then not in the satisfying way of her experience with Brad, Marcia felt that Gene didn't love her and didn't care for her as a person. And Gene, in turn, felt that Marcia didn't care for him because she never asked him for sex or seemed to be very interested when they had sex together. Each seemed to be measuring the other on the basis of sexual compatibility, but they were really struggling with the different role expectations of one for the other. This produced personal conflicts in their feelings about themselves and each other.

Man-woman role pattern is lacking

They had such weak roles as husband and wife that they seldom went out with other persons. They lacked the roles of "man and woman being together," which sometimes happens when the husband-wife pattern is weak. This lack of man-woman role pattern was a direct result of their weak sexual contact.

Finally, Gene began to work through his relationship with Marcia. He realized he cared for her very much, and that he loved her and she could love him too if they could find a way to reach it. He knew that they weren't matched closely in their sexuality, but this was not the determinant in love.

Gene went through what he knew to be his role expectations for Marcia. Most of them didn't fit her. She didn't do things well in the outer world, such as cooking, housekeeping, organizing her life to fit his, and so on. Gene realized that if given a chance, she could find her way to these roles in a manner that fit her. Underneath he had always suspected he could give her this kind of help, if he took the time.

At the first opportunity, Gene urged Marcia to quit her job. He also bought a new home. Marcia had never wanted or liked to work, but had spent most of her life on a job. She had never had time to develop roles that fit her, or even to find out what roles were there for her. Very quickly Marcia started finding roles that fit.

The solution: Build a role pattern of friendship

Gene dropped his old role expectations of Marcia, at least those he was aware of, and encouraged her to find roles that suited her. With a great deal of effort, he got rid of one major role expectation he had that was powerful and hidden and blocking their relationship: he stopped pretending that Marcia believed he was the greatest sexual "experience" in her life. As this surfaced and was dropped, the way was open for Marcia to reach him in a warm and personal self-to-person friendship. Marcia quickly found several roles that she liked: taking care of a home, cleaning, cooking, shopping, owning her own car, finding ways of doing things at her own speed and choice. And underneath this she built with Gene a *basic integrating role of friendship* which he responded to in kind.

There was another component of the relationship between Gene and Marcia that aided this friendship role: Marcia respected and admired many of Gene's abilities. They also shared similar ideals about other persons and the world at large. Although Gene was a verbal, he was a soft verbal. And although Marcia was an anomic, she became an aggressive anomic with her discovery of roles that fit her.

They had moved closer together. The relationship continued to change, however, as will be seen later.

Successful verbal friendship

Two hard verbals, when they are male and female (such as Frank and Teddy), can build a close friendship together. But two hard verbal males or two hard verbal females seldom find friendship. Soft verbal Craig and hard verbal Frank were good friends, just as hard verbal Mac and soft verbal Les became friends, as described earlier.

The closest verbal friendship is found between a hard and a soft verbal, where one of the two can take the lead from time to time. If one must dominate the other, we have the situation of the two gunfighters living in the same town; eventually, one must lose. Verbals enjoy being together in large groups, sharing roles and whatever activity has brought them together. They are more comfortable when they have other verbals around to relate to as colleagues. They must be members of a similar profession or job, social or civic club such as the Elks, Kiwanis, a community committee, and so on. Verbals share friendship through the activity, not with the person who is the friend. The friend has to be identified in the role of whatever the activity is that is shared.

Two soft verbals (such as Craig and Gene) could become close friends. Verbals and anomics seldom can share friendship. Anomics are drawn to verbals out of respect and admiration for the way they cope with the outside world, but this is not friendship. Verbals who are friends do not appear to be friends when viewed by anomics. Verbals seldom have the close person-to-person feeling for one another, as do anomic friends.

Verbals and love

As hard verbal Teddy changed, integrated, and softened from her contact with her baby, she and Frank had a good chance to find love. Verbals do not love in the sense of a deep inner sharing and closeness. Verbals are out of touch with their inner world of feelings and emotions, and love is an emotion that rises from strong feelings.

Verbal love is a sharing of what is being done together, not of being together. Frank and Teddy had a solid verbal friendship, and from this friendship verbal love could derive. But this love is not the same or even similar to what is commonly understood to be love.

If Frank were to die, or to leave Teddy, she would find someone else to fit the roles that Frank filled so adequately for her. The *person* is not as important as *what the person does*. Teddy would have found another physician, perhaps, who had about the same characteristics that she liked in Frank. And she would be just as happy. And the same would be true of Frank looking for a replacement for Teddy.

Verbals feel very much in love when they have well-organized lives together, where they function within a solid structure of planned living, and where the future is determined by past accomplishment.

Hard verbals seldom find any kind of verbal love together. The intense need to compete and dominate never allows a friendship to form, the basis for the deeper love relationship. The most successful verbal love is between a hard and a soft verbal.

As there is little possibility of friendship between verbals and anomics, there is even less possibility for love between these two very different kinds of persons (such as Craig and Joanna). As noted earlier, Joanna would have to become an aggressive anomic before friendship could grow between them. Love was not possible there, if they couldn't be friends first.

Marcia and Gene were an exception to the general incompatibility of verbals and anomics in friendship and love. But Gene was a soft verbal, close to integration, and Marcia was on her way to integrating as an aggressive anomic. This relationship was changing, each person was balancing out, moving toward the center where verbals and anomics touch in integration.

Just as with the sexual act between verbals and anomics, when love does happen between them, it can be one of the more creative of human relationships. Each complements the other's "missing" part. Where the verbal gains a sense of his inner world of emotions, the anomic gets in touch with his outer world. Love for another person as a person comes very hard for a verbal, and the path is extremely painful. A verbal-anomic combination is so rare that it seems frivolous to list it. But when it does happen, it is a very satisfying human relationship.

11

How to Stay in Touch
With Yourself

John was a young man who lived at home with his parents, working days and going to school nights. He got along well with his mother, but he intensely disliked his father. John said very little to his father, and tried to avoid him whenever possible. He was having stomach trouble and headaches, and was physically and mentally tired most of the time. John had a verbal personality, and had over-integrated his roles, his personality of social behavior. This is how he did it:

John disliked his father's personal habits, especially the way he ate at the table. John felt disgust when his father gobbled and smacked his food. Believing that a good son should not feel that way about his father, John ignored the feelings he had about his father's eating habits. So, every day, John had to suppress these feelings whenever he saw his father eat.

The continued suppression of the feelings soon became too painful to keep down. The next step was that John pretended he didn't have these feelings. Then the final step: John decided that his father was responsible for—was the cause of—his feelings because he truly wanted to be a good son, and was not responsible if he was prevented (by his father) from having good feelings about his father.

This is the process of introjection and projection of roles by the verbal personality. It is one of the most misunderstood dynamics in psychology. John learned and introjected, or took in, the role of being a good son as taught by his father and mother, and others around him, without changing the role to fit himself. He then projected this role of being a good son *into his personality* of social behavior. This projection of the role was directed into his personality, not out to the outer world. John adopted this role as his own, but did not absorb the role in his natural behavior. He could not. He did not like his father as a person. The "good son" role did not fit John.

The verbal personality introjects a role intact, projects this role into his personality, and then asks other persons to interact with this role presentation of himself. The person who dresses and acts like Napoleon does not believe that he really is Napoleon, but has introjected, or taken in, the role of Napoleon, and projected it into his personality. He is asking the world then to react to him *as if he were* Napoleon. The projection of Napoleon is not to the outside world, but into the personality, which is artificial and not the real person.

John's problem and its solution

John was not crazy, although he felt like it sometimes. The process of introjecting taught roles, and projecting these roles into a personality of social behavior, is the dynamic of the verbal personality who tends to over-integrate social behavior. John was out of touch with his inner world of feelings and emotions because he tended to by-pass these and relate himself only to the outer world of persons and things around him. He ignored or suppressed his feelings. This is the dynamic of the verbal personality everywhere, whatever the race, color, or nationality.

John was alienated, out of touch with himself and others. He was in a stuck point, an impasse where he couldn't break through and find himself or get in touch with creative processes that would integrate him and make him whole. But

he made progress with the experiments in sensory awareness described in this book (chapter 1). He was trying to get
in touch with himself, and with others. The important thing
for him to learn was how to *stay in touch*, once he knew what
to do to get in touch.

Verbal-anomic differences

The way in which a verbal personality (such as John)
stays in touch with himself differs from that of the anomic.
John had suppressed his feelings in his inner world so long
that his major effort was to discover *what he felt* when he
made contact with the outer world. This meant that in his
eating, eliminating, touching, and sexual sensory contact
experiments, he had to sort out and discover what he was
feeling inside after he made the contact. He made good physical contact with people. He had a firm grasp in his handshake
with a person. When he shook hands, he had to begin to discover what his true feelings were about the other person, and
to let those feelings occur.

The anomic is just the opposite, as may be seen. The
anomic doesn't have a firm grasp in a handshake, and has
many feelings flowing up from the contact. The anomic's
problem is to sort out his feelings to find out which ones
really fit the reaction he is having to the person he is shaking
hands with.

Once John became accustomed to discovering how he
felt inside about the contacts he made with persons or objects
(cars, pencils, shoes, clothes, streets, houses, and so on), his
next step was to find the words that fit these feelings and
speak them out loud to himself. The process of finding words
to fit inner feelings and speaking them out loud is the single
most integrating dynamic in getting and staying in touch
with yourself.

John had breakthroughs very quickly in some areas with
his sensory awareness and contact work. But the persistence
of role behavior is so great that persons may have only temporary success in getting in touch with themselves and soon

backslide unless they *learn to stay in touch* with their natural behavior and responses.

Again, verbal personalities, such as John, have to concentrate on staying in touch with themselves, even after some success in discovering their feelings of their inner world. For instance, John had to rediscover almost daily how he felt about a telephone, that he had a feeling stemming from his contact with it; that he had a feeling, perhaps minor, but a feeling nonetheless about the persons he met casually during the day.

The healing dynamic

The discovery that *he has feelings* then finding words that fit these feelings, is the healing dynamic of the verbal. This in itself, if done regularly, will allow a verbal like John to stay in touch with himself.

This process of integration would differ if John were an anomic, one who tends to under-integrate role behavior, and is out of touch with the outer world. In this case, the healing dynamic would be for John to make good, clear contact with an object (or person), then discover from the variety of feelings he was experiencing what feelings fit the contact he was making.

For example: An anomic might pick up a telephone and respond too soon to several feelings about it, such as dislike of talking over a phone because the other person can't be seen, fear of not knowing what to say, uneasiness about telephones in general, and so on. He has too many feelings. The anomic has to stop, sort through what he is feeling, then find words to describe his exact feelings at the time. Then, he must talk out loud about these feelings. As with the verbal, the finding of words to fit the feelings, and speaking them out loud, is creative integration of the inner and outer worlds of a person. This is how verbals and anomics both stay in touch with themselves.

There are other important ways in which a person may stay in touch with himself. Let me illustrate by describing an anomic girl and how she took in roles. The anomic dynamic is quite different from the verbal.

Marjorie Sue, an anomic, tended to under-integrate roles taught to her. She was absorbed in her inner world, and was out of touch with her outer world of persons and objects. Marjorie Sue's mother taught her the role that a little girl of eight puts on a dress and goes out to play, but doesn't get her dress dirty.

Marjorie Sue thought that was fine because she liked the dress, and she went out to play; but in playing, she always got her dress dirty. She liked to play and forgot her role of keeping her dress clean. Now, Marjorie Sue did not accomplish the first step of role learning, that of introjecting the role. She introjected only part of the taught role, and was confused when she realized she had gotten her dress dirty.

Verbal and anomic compared

Whereas verbal John introjected the whole role of being a good son, then projected this role into his personality intact, and finally tried to adjust his natural behavior to fit this role, Marjorie Sue did not make the first step of introjecting the role at all. This is a fundamental difference between the dynamics of the anomic and verbal personalities. Verbal John tended to over-intergrate his roles; anomic Marjorie Sue tended to under-integrate her roles. Verbal John got out of touch with his inner world because he related to others within his personality of roles. Anomic Marjorie Sue got out of touch with her outer world because she related to her inner world of feelings and emotions rather than her outer world, and she did not have the roles with which to relate to others.

The process of staying in touch for the verbal, then, is persistent contact with how he feels inside about what is going on outside, regardless of what the role script calls for. The process of staying in touch for the anomic is persistent "sorting out of feelings," and finding the ones that fit what is going on at the moment in the outside world.

This process includes different role procedures for the verbal and anomic. A verbal must learn to abandon those roles or parts of roles that do not fit him. For example, John learned that he could be a good son, yet he recognized that his father could be a father but not be likable as a person. Not all fathers are likable people. John took roles too seriously, as if they were the word of truth. Some entire roles and parts of some roles fit John, and he had to learn to adjust these roles to fit his natural behavior and not try to adjust himself to fit the roles.

Anomic Marjorie Sue had to learn to adopt roles long enough to find out what parts fit her, then to practice them and not feel afraid when the role didn't fit. She lived in frustration because she did not understand why her mother couldn't see that she was trying to be a good girl and keep her dresses clean. Marjorie Sue should have had a role that allowed her to wear play clothes when she went out to play. This role would fit her, and allow her to get dirty without feeling badly about it. More than likely, she would keep these play clothes cleaner than she did her dresses, if allowed to adopt a role closer to her real behavior.

Additional ways to stay in touch: Using unpleasant memories and fantasies

There are other ways an anomic or verbal person may stay in touch with himself. I have noted these in earlier chapters but, because they are so very useful for staying in touch after progress has started, I will briefly go over them once more.

One of the surest healing dynamics is to recapture an unpleasant experience in careful detail, and recreate it as if it were occurring for the first time. Recreate the details of the experience and find words to fit the rising feelings as they occur in the present. This recreating of memories in the *now* begins the process of integrating the unfinished emotional reaction that lies underneath that nagging, unpleasant memory.

Unless this old memory is created as if it were occurring now, integration of the past event with the present emotion will not occur. If John, for instance, wanted to integrate his unpleasant memories of his father, he would have to work them through in the following manner:

John sits down and recalls the last most unpleasant experience he had with his father. He lets this happen. The memory will rise on its own thrust because it is not resolved emotionally in his present feelings. He doesn't try to go back to when it happened and think about how he felt *then*. He tries to find out what he is feeling *now* about what happened yesterday, or whenever.

The process of re-creation

John works and re-works through his unpleasant memory of his father sitting at the table, eating, smacking, gobbling his food, pretending that he, John, is now sitting across the table, now watching his father eat. In his mind's eye, John envisions his father—big lips, food flakes on his face, liquid dripping from the corner of his mouth, catsup on his hand, belching. In infinite detail John recreates this scene, allows what he feels now about it to surface and talks out loud, finding words to fit his feelings.

Surging up from underneath a variety of feelings comes disgust. Then John starts getting something else . . . disgust with himself, no . . . under that is a real fear—fear that he is just like his father. He doesn't want to be like his father, but he fears he is. This is a tremendous insight for John, to become aware that much of his dislike for his father stems from his simply wanting to be himself.

This insight—this reworking of an unpleasant memory in the now and the discovery of the emotion underlying it— allowed John to integrate his emotional response so that it could subside and get out of the way, and he could become organized to act in concert with his true feelings. He could eat with his father and not suffer. He still did not like how his father ate, but John accepted his feelings and understood that he felt as he did because he did not want to be like his father. A perfectly normal reaction.

Fantasies and daydreams

On the other side of inner life lies a person's pleasant fantasies and daydreams. These can be used to stay in touch with oneself too. The process is similar to that of recovering unpleasant memories and integrating them.

Marjorie Sue daydreamed (fantasied) a lot. She learned to daydream or fantasy (they are synonomous) in the *present,* not as if the fantasy would occur at some future time, or had occurred in the past. She learned to daydream about herself doing things with her mother and father as if she were doing them *now,* that is, at the moment. She pretended she and her parents were going on a picnic together, now driving in the car together, now flying in the car over the country and landing beside a quiet stream.

Marjorie Sue was encouraged to find words to fit her feelings during her fantasy, however funny or crazy. She found that she did not think her father loved her as much as he loved her mother, but on picnics he seemed to love Marjorie Sue more because he played and talked with her. Once this was verbally expressed, Marjorie Sue could identify her feeling and the emotional need underlying her fantasy.

Then she could talk it over with her dad. Her father was able to respond to this and express his love for her. He reassured her that he loved her equally as much as he did her mother, but perhaps in a different way because they were different persons.

Underneath each and every fantasy lies an unresolved emotional need. The best way to stay in touch with yourself is to discover and identify the unresolved emotional needs that give impetus to your pleasant thoughts, your fantasies. Again, these must be created in the present, as if they were occurring now, and not at some time in the future or past.

The integration will not occur, nor will there be insight into the underlying emotion, if the person pretends the event is happening sometime in the future or in the past. The unresolved emotional need is *current*. It is occurring at the moment of the daydream, and does not have a past or a future. Inner emotional needs are always in the present. Feelings and emotions are constantly changing, moving along in the present inner life of a person and have no relevance to what has occurred in the past or might occur in the future.

The inner life, the emotions, want resolution *now,* so that the underlying need can subside and get out of the way for the next emerging need and its accompanying emotional response. If a person is in touch with this inner dynamic, he *stays in touch with himself.*

The verbal person tends to live in the past, using old behavior to satisfy current needs. The anomic tends to live in the future, wanting some future behavior to satisfy current needs. The dynamic of needs and emotions is going on in both, always in their present behavior. It takes practice to overcome long role habits to stay in touch with yourself.

Keystone of personality: Sex typed roles

The only way a person can pretend to live in the past, as verbals do, or in the future, as anomics do, is to adopt roles that allow this complex pretense. It is artificial behavior, not the genuine natural behavior of the person. How does this happen? How have millions come to believe that their personality is their real behavior? If roles are alienating and unhealthy, how can so many persons, everywhere, be doing the same things with themselves?

The answer seems straightforward: In order for persons to come together in large groups they must learn to restrain their natural impulses and defer to the needs of other individuals in the group. The larger the group, the more restraints in behavior are needed to accommodate individual differences. These behavior restraints, or curbs, are set down everywhere as roles, the accepted group ways of doing things. How does a society transmit its desired restraints to so many individuals? The restraints are spelled out in specific role patterns and taught to individuals as rights, duties, obligations, and privileges owed to other persons, who in turn have some reciprocal responsibility.

But in order for a person to adopt roles that channel his behavior, there must be a strong inner need to which the behavior is attached so that the role can be internalized, that is, taken in and used as social behavior to replace the natural behavior of the person.

Healthy dynamic disturbed

Modern (and most ancient) societies have attached role behavior to the sexual impulse and this is the keystone of an individual's personality. All roles are sex typed, with specific ways of doing things as a male or female. Whenever a person reacts or responds to another, or to an object, he has had to learn to respond as a male or female should respond as defined by his culture. This may not seem unhealthy, and may even appear normal. But think a moment. If you are hungry, you satisfy this need by eating. If you first adjust yourself to fit the manners of the way a male or a female eats, you warp your genuine response to a genuine need. The healthy dynamic has been disturbed.

By sex-typing all the roles, pretending that things are done always as a female or male and not as a person who may be male or female, every single action of the person is modified and incomplete. The inner dynamic of "need-emotion-response to need" is channeled through the sexual impulse, whether or not it has any remote connection with the person's sexuality.

Marjorie Sue had great difficulty taking on sex-typed roles that defined her behavior as different from males, when daily she felt she was sharing behavior common to both males and females. She was not yet aware of her sexuality. But she had pink booties waiting for her when she was born.

This sex-typing of roles begins at birth and there is no specific sexual behavior to control for many years. By the time the person reaches sexual age, his sexuality is so thoroughly buried in role behavior unrelated to sexual responses that he feels alienated and disconnected from himself and the world around him. He is fascinated with things sexual beyond all apparent reason. His personality is artificial and keyed to his sexuality. This unhealthy sex-typing of roles, implanting roles on the sexual impulse, and hooking them into this strong human drive, keeps the person off balance in gratifying all his other needs.

He must learn the accepted group ways of behaving to get love, affection, shelter, food and protection. He must learn the roles to satisfy his survival needs. This is the way social control of the individual is exerted in modern societies, whatever the politics, and wherever man comes together in large numbers for complex behavior.

Marjorie Sue already knew there were visible biological differences between her and males. She was learning that girls *behave* differently from boys — that girls *should, ought, must, have to behave* differently from boys, as taught in roles. Boys don't wear dresses. Boys can get dirty. Girls wear dresses and shouldn't get them dirty.

Reasons for Marjorie Sue's problem

Marjorie Sue didn't understand this sex-typed difference in behavior and this caused her great difficulty in adopting roles that fit her, or any roles at all. She was an anomic person, and tended to under-integrate social behavior. This tendency was magnified because her roles were keyed to her sexuality, and not to her current needs as a young person who happened to be a girl. Like virtually everyone, she had difficulty developing a personality, and in her case, as an anomic, she tended to under-integrate social behavior.

The verbal has the problem of "taking in whole" entire roles, even though they have little relevance to his needs. John swallowed whole the male role of being a good son, believing that being a good son was the only male way to be. It caused him great pain. Being a person who happens to be a son has nothing to do with being a good or bad male. But that's the way it was keyed in John's personality; that's the way he introjected the role, then projected it into his outer behavior, where it became his personality.

Sexual expression and roles

This sex-typing of roles, where the person learns to adjust himself to others *as a male or female,* regardless of how he feels or fits the role, does work as social control of individuals. From the time persons are born, and throughout their early childhood, they learn to adjust themselves to behavior that is not appropriate to their needs. All through these years they are adjusting themselves to become well-adjusted personalities as young males or females, sex-typed, without any feeling of *sexuality* about the behavior.

Marjorie Sue didn't feel she was a sexual person; she felt that she was a girl who did things in certain specified ways according to what she had been told was proper. By the time she gets to be a sexually aware person, she will already have created a personality for herself keyed to a sexuality she never had. She may buy toothpaste, get a new hairdo, buy clothes, learn new dances, all with the anticipation that she can find female sexual expression in these activities, because she has learned to do them as female roles. These roles have nothing to do with her genuine sexuality. Eventually she may be fascinated by all the books and movies and pictures and jokes that touch on this unresolved need to find direct sexual expression outside role behavior.

These sex-keyed roles teach persons to be regulated by others, not to regulate themselves. They teach persons to adjust to fit the needs of others, not to find others who fit their own unique needs. By the time Marjorie Sue is twenty, she may come to believe that her personality of roles is her real self. She will have responded so long to the personality trap that she may believe her discontent and unhappiness with herself is natural.

Verbals such as John need to *discard roles* (or parts of roles) that don't fit them. He had too many roles supporting his verbal personality. Anomic Marjorie Sue had to learn to *adopt new roles,* to practice them and keep those that fit her. This process of finding roles or discarding roles usually is a long term process for persons, especially after they enter their twenties, and even more so when they are embedded in dependent relationships with others who are locked into role obligations with them.

Finding the roles that fit

Incredible as it may seem, it would not take great effort to get most persons started along the way to personal integration. If people were encouraged to learn to *find the roles that fit them* from the broad array available in every human effort, the healthy dynamic would begin. This involves the imperative that the individual must be informed and aided in finding and making the choices of roles that fit his own genuine behavior. He then could find play roles, work roles, sex roles, friendship roles, love roles, and all the other roles that fit him and he could absorb them as his own. He could abandon his artificial personality and creatively respond to others, and to his and their inner needs.

This is the dynamic of mental and physical health. There are several ways — roles — for being a good son, a good daughter, a good husband or wife or worker or what have you, and persons should be encouraged to find those that fit them best. There is *never* just one way to do things, never just one role.

The way it is, all the social pathologies increase each year, and will continue to increase as more and more persons stay out of touch with themselves. This is painful. Drug and alcohol use, and crime and violence will mount, get ever greater.

Another and perhaps significant speculation seems appropriate as a result of the relentless sex-keyed personality: More and more persons unable to integrate their social behavior with their natural behavior will not only develop stronger anomic or stronger verbal personalities, but more and more males and females, especially males, will turn to homosexuality in an attempt to find satisfactory sex, friendship, and love relationships.

Appendix

The Group Phenomenon

Although a description of how the small group phenomenon grew is not essential to the understanding and use of
this book, the author is aware that at least some readers may
be interested. Therefore, a brief outline is offered herewith.

The small group phenomenon, which is one of the more
significant revolutions shaping conventional psychology
today, has captured the imagination of many people in the
United States. It appears to answer the yearnings, forgotten
or suppressed, of people to gather in groups as a means for
emotional release and renewal.

The academic psychologist has been slow to react, apparently treating the phenomenon as if it were a fad, and assuming that it would soon fade away. The applied psychologists,
more responsive to popular demands in the marketplace, are
attempting to fill the gap with the wide variety of "pop"
group forms that have proliferated with perhaps as many
different methods as there are practitioners.

T-groups, sensitivity groups, encounter groups, marathon
groups, learning groups, transaction-analysis groups, Esalen
groups, and so on and on — shifting titles in a maze of applications. There is a reason for this apparent lack of consis-
tency. Psychology was caught short in its knowledge of small

group behavior when the phenomenon appeared in the late 1940s. There was no foundation, no real theoretical underpinnings of scientific information, about human behavior in small groups of two to fifteen or twenty persons.

This remarkable oversight most probably is one result of psychology's studied disinterest in a person's emotions and feelings, his *affective* behavior. A person's inner environment is, of course, disordered, unpredictable and difficult if not impossible to measure in any "scientific" way under neat laboratory conditions.

Game groups and growth groups

The variety and confusion of the small group phenomenon was and is predictable and will continue. The multitude of methods still moves along because of the lack of general knowledge about the structure and function of small group behavior. This lack of knowledge is most apparent in two clearly identifiable trends: *game groups* and *growth groups*. These two trends seem to be the outgrowth of the confusion and lack of agreement and understanding of the underlying structural and functional properties of human behavior in small groups.

In undoubtedly a too simplistic description, a game group emphasizes the structure of the group, and a growth group stresses the group's function. In a game group there is an authority, a leader who structures the group situation with tasks, things to do, ends to gain, and games to play. Much attention is paid to group characteristics such as similarities of occupation of the members, or marital status, or age, or some other biographical description.

In a growth group, function is stressed. Authoritarian leadership gives way to "leaderlessness" and participation rests upon voluntary responses emerging from individuals. An attempt is made to create an atmosphere of openness with little overt guidance from a professional expert.

Both game and growth groups may lead to disaster when either is limited to a certain approach. Game groups soon

suffer from the press of conformity which cannot be concealed when everyone is asked — or required — to do the same
things, even though it may be as interesting as taking off
their clothes for a dip in a pool or a romp through the clover.
The emotions generated by games can be powerful but their
rapid decay after the sessions may dishearten participants.
One of the more common criticisms of game members is
that no lasting personality change, or growth, really occurs.

A quite different problem seems to beset growth groups.
Most person are uneasy and anxious when faced with situations where they are urged to explore their feelings on their
own, undirected. They feel ambiguous, open, and vulnerable
when pressed to seek personal autonomy in a relatively
undefined atmosphere.

The more traditional psychologist or psychiatrist, or
similar professional, tends to be more comfortable with
game groups, while the less orthodox (or wilder) enthusiasts
appear to find a better fit with growth-oriented groups.

In any respect, what we do *not* know (or cannot agree
upon) about small group behavior is staggering: Who should
be in a group? Who shouldn't? How many make up the best
group? How long should they last? What should they do?
Who should run a group, if anyone? What kind of training,
if any, qualifies a group leader? What is a group? This list
appears endless.

Underneath this sound there are furies of real disagreement. Psychologists are not all in agreement on the very
order of responses of a person. This is not a subtle academic
difference of opinion but a gross argument. Many psychologists maintain that perception, thought, and thinking *precede*
feelings and emotional response; others insist on the reverse
— that you feel, or sense, a stimulus prior to cognition.

Game groups are built on the assumption that your feelings follow perception, and growth groups operate on the belief that inner feelings must precede thought and action.
Consider the difference: If you are offered a way to control
your thoughts, it is assumed you can then control your feel-

ings. Or, if you are presented a way to control your feelings, you can then control your thoughts.

It is most probable that both of these formulas are false or at best inadequate prescriptions. This apparent basic difference perhaps conceals a deeper argument for which there is increasing positive evidence: That the structure and function of small group behavior are interrelated and simultaneous and that individual feelings and thoughts are determined by this interaction, whatever the order. These are some of the problems to be explored.

Gestalt psychology has a long history but it has never enjoyed much attention from most of the American brands of psychology. What has held the greatest attraction could be described as the more traditional divisions of Behavioristic and Freudian psychologies. These two currents have dominated academic teaching, textbooks, and applied psychology through most of the history of America. But there are serious gaps in both of these approaches to the psychology of human behavior.

The Behaviorists have maintained a pristine aloofness toward the individual's emotional world. Feelings do not lend themselves to easy measurement or even identification. For example, love, sadness, and happiness do not have accurate yardsticks. Therefore, as stated in one of the more obscure scientific postures: What cannot be measured is not the concern of the scientist. Part of the problem, undoubtedly, is that humans are difficult to experiment with under laboratory conditions.

Freudian psychology suffers from a quite different shortcoming. It tends to view man through pathological lenses, through his inner conflicts, with the assumption that these are the major determinants of behavior. It holds that most if not all behavior is imbedded in the dynamics of that trio of antagonists, the id, ego, and superego.

Always, there have been some psychologists who have objected to the limitations of both the Behaviorist and Freudian theories. This small band, sometimes called Third Force

Psychology, or the New Wave Psychologists, is gaining increasing attention. The popularity of the small group phenomenon is boosting the recognition of the Third Force Psychologists who insist that the proper study of psychology begins with man's affective world, his emotions and feelings; and that these are founded in strong biological strivings for creative growth and change. Several schools or philosophies have influenced the Third Force in psychology: phenomenology, existentialism, humanism, and gestalt, to name the more prominent.

Gestalt psychology has had a erratic growth under the dominance of the Behavioristic and Freudian schools. It has been blessed with a minor rebirth of interest with the advent of the small group phenomenon and the popular success of centers such as Esalen in California.

Gestalt is a German word; as a verb, it means to form, to fashion, or to take shape or turn out. Gestalt psychology is concerned with the unity, the nature of the totality of responses involved in human behavior as opposed to the fragmentation into isolated stimulus-response patterns of the Behaviorists or the analysis of separate motivating forces of the Freudians.

Gestalt emphasizes the *integrative* patterns of human behavior as against the *reduction* of behavior into parts. Gestalt insists that the sum of human behavior is different from and determines its parts, and that attempts to reduce it destroy its meaning. Gestalt puts its strongest emphasis on the positive components of growth and change in human behavior. This is a fundamental difference in emphasis — affective as opposed to cognitive forms of behavior.

Suggested Readings

Barron, Frank, *Creative Person and Creative Process*. Holt, Rinehart and Winston, Inc., New York, 1969.

Bonner, Hubert, *On Being Mindful of Man*. Houghton Mifflin Company, Boston, 1965.

Jourard, Sidney, *Disclosing Man to Himself*. Van Nostrand Company, Inc., New York, 1968.

Murphy, Gardner, *Human Potentialities*. Basic Books, New York, 1958.

Perls, Frederick S., with Ralph Hefferline and Paul Goodman, *Gestalt Therapy: Excitement and Growth in the Human Personality*, Dell Publishing Co., New York, 1951.

Perls, Frederick S., *Gestalt Therapy Verbatim*. Real People Press, Lafayette, California, 1969.

Rogers, Carl R., *On Becoming a Person*. Houghton Mifflin Company, Boston, 1961.

Index-Glossary

anomic, 27. *From the French word, anomie, meaning "normlessness."*
anomic personality, 27, 54-55. *Personality of one who tends to under-integrate social behavior transmitted as roles; lacking in sufficient roles.*
aggressive and weak compared, 204-205
anticipating feelings, 48
based on friendship role, 202, 203-207
compared with verbal, 62-63, 71-75, 109, 111, 137, 162, 186-188, 233-234
conversational traits of, 139
determining if one has, 32-33, 138-139
enjoyment of other anomics, 205
example of, 36-41
extreme, 37
finding love by, 208-210
in artificial groups, 31-32
penalized by achievement tests, 165-166
percent of people with, 38, 199

school problems of, 166-169
successful friendships of, 211
artificial group, 14-15, 29-32. *Any gathering of persons wherein the primary relationships require formal role interaction as contrasted with informal, personal care for the members of the group.*
goals of, 151
shift from natural group to, 41, 42
affective behavior, 248. *Those responses that involve the rise of sensation from inner or outer stimuli, and expand into feelings and on into emotional responses. The affective response precedes and organizes the cognitive response. Affective behavior is a roleless response.*
basic integrating role. *A role that fits a person's natural behavior and unifies the social role with natural responses. This basic role is*